SHEPHERDING CARE

The Church and Church Membership

Recovering a Biblical Ecclesiology

JOHN MACARTHUR

The Church and Church Membership: Recovering a Biblical Ecclesiology
The Christian Life Series

Published by CLC Publications

USA: P.O. Box 1449, Fort Washington, PA 19034
www.clcpublications.com

UK: Kingsway CLC Trust
Unit 5, Glendale Avenue, Sandycroft, Flintshire, CH5 2QP
www.equippingthechurch.com

ISBN (paperback): 978-1-61958-390-0
ISBN (ebook): 978-1-61958-391-7

Printed in the United States of America

Italics in Scripture quotations, if not original to the NASB, are the emphasis of the author.

PRAISE FOR
THE CHURCH AND CHURCH MEMBERSHIP
AND JOHN MACARTHUR

"This book has come at a key moment in church history. Society today has infiltrated many churches in ways that lead to confusion among leaders and discontentment among members. John MacArthur provides much needed clarity and insight into how an 'ordinary church' is truly extraordinary. This book will not only help remind leaders to remain on task, but it will help every member to grow in his or her love for the body of Christ, 'the fullness of Him who fills all in all' (Eph. 1:23). John MacArthur has produced a work that should not only increase your love for Christ, but as you consider these chapters, they will invigorate your desire to serve the body with increased joy."

— Brian Biedebach, Dean of Students and Associate Professor of Pastoral Ministry, The Master's Seminary

The Church and Church Membership is a necessary appeal to professing believers in Jesus Christ to recapture the church's true *raison d'etre*—its reason and purpose for existing. Leveraging historical doctrinal distinctives that comprise the church's spiritual and ecclesiastical DNA, this book is a timely and challenging reminder to believers and unbelievers alike that the mission of the church remains firm and unwavering regardless of the direction the uncertain winds of culture may blow.

— Darrell B. Harrison, Shepherding and Teaching Pastor, Redeemer Bible Church, Gilbert, AZ

"Dr. MacArthur's preaching is incredibly clear. He has the ability to relate the immediacy of the text to doctrinal concerns or cultural concerns without getting off on a tangent."

—John Piper, Founder and teacher of Desiring God, Chancellor of Bethlehem College and Seminary

"John MacArthur has proven himself to be a sure guide through Scripture and a faithful expositor of God's Word."

—R. Albert Mohler, JR., President, Southern Baptist Theological Seminary

"With the possible exception of Dr. Tim LaHaye, no other Bible commentator has informed my own writing as much as that of John MacArthur. I find myself turning to him again and again."

—Jerry B. Jenkins, author of The Left Behind series

"For decades John MacArthur has exemplified expository preaching, putting on full display the Word of God for the people of God."

—Matthew Barrett, Tutor of Systematic Theology and Church History, Oak Hill Theological College

Titles in the Christian Life Series

Published in 2023

Heaven and Hell: A Survey of the Biblical Doctrines of Personal Eschatology (Kevin Zuber)

The Forgotten Attributes of God: God's Nature and Why It Matters (Peter Sammons)

Old Testament Survey I: Genesis to Esther (Nathan LeMaster)

Well Done: A Strategy for Life Stewardship (Reagan Rose)

Becoming a Worthy Reader: How to Read and Study the Bible (Kevin Zuber)

Published in 2024

New Testament Survey I: Matthew to Acts & Johannine Literature (Nathan LeMaster)

Gender and Sexuality (Michael Riccardi)

Coming in 2025 (tentative titles)

The Church and Church Membership (John MacArthur)

Old Testament Survey II (Nathan LeMaster)

Salvation and Sanctification (author TBD)

The Spiritual Disciplines (author TBD)

Coming in 2026 and beyond (tentative titles)

Spiritual Leadership (author TBD)

The Creeds of the Church (author TBD)

New Testament Survey II (Nathan LeMaster)

Spiritual Gifts and Service (author TBD)

The Person of God or *The Authority of Scripture* (author TBD)

Biblical Reconciliation (author TBD)

Marriage and Family Counseling (author TBD)

Discipling and Mentoring (author TBD)

Global and Local Missions (author TBD)

Contents

Foreword

IN THE REALM OF evangelical stalwarts, Pastor John MacArthur stands as a towering figure, a beacon of unwavering conviction for the truth of God's Word. His tenure at Grace Community Church since 1969, a remarkable 55 years, speaks volumes about his steadfast commitment to shepherding a congregation. As the Chancellor of The Master's University and Seminary and the voice behind the globally broadcast Grace to You radio program, Pastor John's influence extends far beyond the walls of his church.

While Pastor John's extensive contributions, including a comprehensive commentary on the entire New Testament, have been well-documented, this book unveils a facet often overlooked—his profound ecclesiology. In an era where the definition and function of the church have been distorted by extreme pragmatism, Pastor John emerges as a beacon of timeless wisdom, offering answers rooted in Scripture.

This isn't a mere handbook on ecclesiastical praxis. Instead, it serves as a guide to adopting a God-honoring approach in establishing and defining a faithful congregation amid the challenges of a sin-perverted world. As Martin Luther cautioned, "For where God built a church, there the Devil would also build a chapel." In today's landscape, not everything claiming the title of a church embodies health or truth. Pastor John's book becomes a vital tool for believers, providing a lens to scrutinize the ordinary church in their time.

Amidst the cacophony of modern church culture, replete with noise, fog machines, and strobe lights, Pastor John MacArthur beckons us back to the simplicity of the Ordinary Church. Cutting through the distractions, he invites us to walk the old paths, where the timeless truths of Scripture guide us in discerning what truly constitutes a faithful congregation. Prepare to embark on a journey that transcends the superficial and leads us to the heart of genuine, enduring fellowship.

Peter Sammons, PhD
Author of *Reprobation and God's Sovereignty*
and *The Forgotten Attributes of God*

Introduction

The Church Under Fire

THE CHURCH TODAY—that is, the church in the early part of the twenty-first century—exists at a unique window of time in its history. For the last two to three centuries, the church has been at relative peace with the world. Thanks to the dominance of Judeo-Christian ethics and morality throughout the Western world—and their widespread acceptance beyond—the church has enjoyed a kind of ceasefire in its otherwise near-constant conflict with world powers and social movements.

But that window appears to be closing.

No longer will the biblical authority and restraining influence of the church in the world be tolerated. No more will it shape the moral standards of society. The opposition and persecution that many have predicted for years—and that we see as the consistent norm throughout the rest of church history—is finally here.

Throwing Off the Restraints

The widespread immorality, violence, and social chaos of the last few years indicate the church's waning influence in society. But that upheaval truly began long before. Decade after decade of *détente*, or the relaxation of strained tensions, with the world did not make the church any more skilled in wielding the weapons of our warfare. If anything, many Christians were lulled into a false sense of security and even the delusion of victory, as though mere behavior modification were the goal of Christ's church and the intent of His gospel. They forgot that "God sees not as man sees, for man looks at the outward appearance, but the Lord looks at the heart" (1 Sam. 16:7).

Others acted as though the goals were prominence and popularity with the world, and they were happy to tailor the message and their ministry to suit the tastes of the unregenerate. But shaving off the sharp edges of the gospel doesn't win souls to Christ; it shows them where you're already willing to compromise and where they still need to exert pressure.

The fact that so many churches have compromised and even capitulated to the worldly seduction reveals that there never really was a ceasefire—the world merely took a different approach in its war with the church. The world saw that many churches shifted their focus—that they would settle for social influence alone, and that they were content to create generations of false believers and hypocrites. And so the world played along, lulling the church into thinking it had a far greater preserving influence on society than it truly did.

What many have perceived as the recent explosion of immorality, lewdness, and anarchic behavior is really just the world tearing down the façade and announcing that the charade is over (Ps. 2:1–3). The church diminished its own restraining influence over time—now it's being rejected altogether. That was evident in the years of rioting and violence we've recently endured, and it's evident in the general tone and tenor of the culture today.

Through generations of neglecting its duty to boldly proclaim the truth of Scripture, the church negated its own restraining influence. The church will face difficulties trying to reestablish it.

Public Persecution

It's no coincidence that at the same time society was melting down, governments throughout the Western world relaunched their campaigns of persecuting the church. The attack many of them instituted recently was to simply shut down the church with oppressive COVID–19 restrictions. In Southern California, liquor stores and marijuana dispensaries could open, but churches had to stay closed indefinitely.

For our failure to comply, Grace Community Church faced heavy fines and a lengthy litigation. I know pastors in Canada who were thrown in prison for faithfully continuing to gather with their congregations and preaching the truth that Christ, not Caesar, is the head of the church (Eph. 1:22; Col. 1:18). And even though we were ultimately vindicated in court, we know rulers and officials will continue to find ways to exert authority over the church, which belongs to God alone.

This has been normal throughout church history. Governments are rarely content with overseeing the secular matters of life; they want to ride roughshod over spiritual matters, too. When government leaders can't control the church, they will do everything they can to stamp out its influence altogether.

We're beginning to see signs of that, as once-democratic governments become heavy-handed and authoritarian. We see it in the form of hate speech laws that criminalize the expression of biblical truth—laws that try to force believers to play along with the culture's gender-bending insanity and sexual deviancy. Some believers are already facing the consequences for offending others with the truth. For not playing along with the world's sick and twisted pronoun game, some have lost their jobs, while others are subject to fines and even jail time. We can expect much more of the same, as the world works to establish and protect all forms of immoral corruption.

The church routinely faces opposition on many fronts. Because governments have the power to punish, severe persecution always comes from the state, as they seek to rule in the realm where Christ alone is King. God's people will be tested in the days ahead, as the church falls further out of favor with the world and becomes an easier and more acceptable target for government oppression and opposition.

Digital Distractions

Don't think for a moment that the church is facing only external threats. Today an all-out assault is on its design—a kind of spiritual self-sabotage—from those who claim to know and love the Lord.

I'm talking about the development of digital congregations; the rise of the "meta-church," as its proponents call it.

For years, technological advances have chipped away at church attendance. It began with "flat screen" churches—networks of congregations all viewing the same sermon, or at least the same pastor, from satellite locations. The trend was seen as a way to maintain the small-church feel while sitting under a big-name pastor. It allowed people to attend the local branch of a megachurch. But that is a meager benefit for the cost of corrupting God's design for the church—the sheep cannot be led by a shepherd who will never know them.

The trend expanded as many churches streamed their services live online. It may have been well-intentioned, but it has given license to believers who would rather stay home and watch from the comfort of their couches. But that turns the church service into a spectator sport—one in which the viewer is passive and aloof. That's not how God demands to be worshipped.

Others would argue that livestream services allow them to tune in to other churches and enrich their experience by greater variety from week to week. Livestreaming is useful if it doesn't become a substitute for the local gathering of the church.

I'm convinced many people start with good intentions, but let their commitment to the local church wane over time. Others grow weary looking for a local congregation that meets their standards and settle for following their favorite preachers from afar, forfeiting most of the blessings and benefits of belonging to a church, not to mention the blessings of obedience, in the process.

But the latest innovation in digital congregations is even more distracting and destructive to the body of Christ. Users of digital meeting software and virtual reality have created web-based "congregations" made entirely of strangers who have never met. In some of these meta-churches, the individual is nothing more than a cartoon avatar and a screen name. It reduces the life of the church to a weekly chatroom and the role of the pastor to that of a media performer.

This distorts God's design for His church. The church is by definition an assembly—that is the literal meaning of the Greek word *ekklēsia*. An assembly that does not assemble is a contradiction in terms. Moreover, it's in direct defiance to the clear instruction of Hebrews 10:25, to "not [forsake] our own assembling together, as is the habit of some, but encouraging one another; and all the more as you see the day drawing near."

Worse still, the purveyors of these meta-churches encourage followers to pick and choose congregations and sermons based on their individual tastes and interests. That makes the believer sovereign over his or her church experience—he or she submits to no one, and need never be confronted by any truth he or she doesn't want to hear.

In a sense, this is nothing new for the church. Consumer-driven tactics abound, in hopes of drawing a crowd and building an audience. This is just the latest in a series of tactics to appeal to the world by giving it what it wants rather than what it needs.

And in the case of the meta-church, this individualistic, self-styled approach is a cancer to the true church. It turns the worship of our Lord and Savior into something more akin to a role-playing game and severs believers from their only source of fellowship, discipleship, and accountability. In short, it needlessly carves up the body of Christ.

Applauding Apostasy

I want to draw your attention to another threat from within the church today—one that greatly grieves my heart. You may have heard the term "Christian deconstruction" or encountered people who refer to themselves as "exvangelicals." You might have seen the hashtag #emptythepews online. It's a trend that has gained attention on social media, and people who once professed faith in Christ and allegiance to His church are now rejecting Him, along with the authority of His shepherds and His Word. In essence, it is the popularization of apostasy.

We see a proliferation of false Christianity in our time, and a continual defection of many who once called themselves Christians. In fact, I don't think it's ever been as tempting to abandon the church as it is today, because being a defector from Christianity carries with it the cultural cachet of victimization heroism.

Today, you can go on the Internet and find thousands of people who will applaud a defector as a hero—the same way the world applauds and encourages those caught up in transgenderism or any of the world's other destructive lies. You can even go to conferences that celebrate those who have disavowed biblical Christianity and abandoned the faith.

These defections are certainly not happening because people are studying the Bible deeply and carefully, digging into the Scripture, and coming to the conclusion that the Bible isn't true. That doesn't happen. This is not the product of taking theology seriously or the careful study of sound doctrine.

Rather, the explanation you hear is this: "I had a bad experience at church." "Somebody was unkind to me." "I felt mistreated, ignored, and abused." "I didn't feel safe, cared for, or seen."

It comes down to what everything comes down to in this selfish, worldly culture: the insatiable god of self. That tells me they were initially attracted to the church for some self-satisfying purpose, and when they couldn't find the satisfaction they craved, they blamed and abandoned the church. The bottom line is they love themselves.

I've been a pastor long enough to see fruitless soils that looked good for a while, but weeds choked out what appeared to be spiritual life. Some of the most dramatic testimonies I've heard turned out to be false. And some people weren't discovered as phonies for years, until they finally couldn't hold up the façade any longer, and their love of sin turned them away. Luke 8:13 says of such people, "They believe for a while, and in time of temptation fall away." They're half-converted. They can't withstand tribulation or temptation; they can't loosen their grip on the world—and particularly their favorite transgressions.

Through the years of preaching God's Word, I have come across many passages that should act as warnings to those kinds of people.

One particularly powerful example comes to us in First Corinthians 10. Paul wrote, "For I do not want you to be unaware, brethren, that our fathers were all under the cloud and all passed through the sea," referring to Israel's deliverance from Egypt, "and all were baptized into Moses in the cloud and in the sea" (1 Cor. 10:1–2). They "all ate the same spiritual food"—they received the manna God delivered on a daily basis, "and all drank the same spiritual drink, for they were drinking from a spiritual rock which followed them; and the rock was Christ" (10:3–4).

But even through all that shared experience as the people of God, Paul wrote, "Nevertheless, with most of them God was not well-pleased; for they were laid low in the wilderness" (10:5). They made it out of Egypt, but never entered the Promised Land. They illustrate the half-converted—those who had religious feelings but not true salvation.

Paul told us, "These things happened as examples for us, so that we would not crave evil things as they also craved" (10:6). The people who forsake God, who once may have professed to believe in Him, do so because they crave something more than Him (10:7). They crave evil things, and they "act immorally" (10:8). Such are an example of the disaster of apostasy—when having received the privilege of hearing the truth and being with the people of God, they turn their backs and walk away from the Lord.

Paul concluded in verse 12, "Therefore let him who thinks he stands take heed that he does not fall." You don't want to fall away. Be sure your salvation is genuine, not the delusion of false faith that will draw you away from Christ to abandon His church.

CULTIVATING A LOVE FOR THE CHURCH

I confess I love the church. It's the center of my life and has been since childhood. My father was the pastor of a church when I was born—I grew up in the church. It's the place where I was led to the knowledge of God, where I learned about the person and work of Christ, and where I gained the knowledge of saving and sanctifying truth. It's where I learned how to pray, how to sing, how to worship, how to love, and how to serve. And in the church, I experienced the leading of the Spirit of God, directing me to a life of ministry.

I met my wife in the church. We raised our children in the church, and our grandchildren and great-grandchildren are being raised there, too. It's where I've made lifelong friends and partners in ministry. The church touches every part of my life. In fact, you could say it is my life.

People sometimes ask me why I write so much about issues in the church—why I can't just be quiet and enjoy my ministry. The answer is, I love the church so much that I can't stand by and watch it struggle. I want to help it be all God intended it to be. I love the church too much to do anything else.

I hope this book stimulates a similar affection for the church in your heart; that it encourages you to pour yourself into your local congregation with fresh energy and a deepened commitment to serving in and with the body of Christ. And I hope that, in spite of the church's flaws and difficulties, you come away with a renewed understanding of God's design for His church, and a vigorous, motivating love for the role He has set aside for you in it.

1

Recovering the Ordinary Church

Awesome HAS TO BE ONE of the most overused words in our popular vernacular. It is casually ascribed to the mundane and the mediocre. Some of it has to do with the cultural push, often via social media, to elevate one's life and experiences in comparison to everyone else. But if the commonplace is awesome, then nothing truly is.

We've similarly worn out and abused other words, such as extreme, epic, and explosive. Once those otherwise-useful words start creeping into promotional materials for beverages and corn chips, you know they've lost all intended meaning.

Today, the same thing is happening with the church. Words like radical, breakthrough, and revolutionary are scattered haphazardly throughout the evangelical landscape. Popular churches desire to qualify as "edgy" or "alternative"—they promise to take religious experience to a "whole new level," whatever that means. Why do churches need to market themselves as experientially trendsetting or groundbreaking? Can they all be uniquely extraordinary in their own way?

When did the ordinary church become the enemy?

Overlooking the Ordinary

Where did this evangelical obsession with the radical, revolutionary, and alternative come from? We live in a culture of extremes, but the original fountainhead of this trend toward trendiness goes back much further, to the American revivalism of the 1800s, and in particular, the ministry of Charles Finney. Finney felt that religion, to be valid, had to incorporate some kind of high-impact, high-energy emotional element. His revivals included methods, feelings, experiences, and sentimentalism—which diminished the role of sound exposition and theology.

In this way, gradual spiritual growth, through the normal, ordinary means of grace, including prayer, Bible study, and fellowship, was exchanged for radical experiences, and the evangelical world had been introduced to a restless search for something extreme.

Churches today are living out that insatiable search, and as a result, they are mired in restlessness, impatience, and selfishness. In a word, that kind of church has become childish. The modern church is a perpetual adolescent, craving to be indulged and entertained. It is largely superficial and immature, devising experiences for impatient, selfish, shallow adolescents.

The God-ordained ordinary patterns of slow, faithful, thoughtful study and absorption of the Word of God, along with steady growth in grace and the knowledge of Christ in the midst of a faithful congregation, are far too humdrum for those who crave a radical, explosive, mystical, or emotional experience. And frankly, so many charlatans are out there promising the extreme and the extraordinary that the ordinary means of grace—not to mention the ordinary churches—seem dull by comparison. So many of every generation in the church have been raised to think that spirituality is nothing more than untamed emotions, resulting in a plethora of spiritual adolescents chasing after the next wild, new experience.

I'm not saying that God Himself is ordinary. God is decidedly not ordinary. But He does work extraordinarily through ordinary means. He uses ordinary people in ordinary churches, doing very ordinary things. God uses real language and ordinary folks as His instruments to move His ordinary church to high impact in the world. Even Jesus—God incarnate—stayed nine months in His mother's womb and was born the ordinary way in a very ordinary place. He grew "in wisdom and stature, and in favor with God and men" in an ordinary, human way (Luke 2:52).

That holds no interest for many churches today. They're chasing the next experience that will catapult them to the next emotional level, without understanding that they're mistaking momentary sensory highs for spiritual growth. Such things don't satisfy God's true people. They won't endure it for long.

We need to be reintroduced to the ordinary church. And the best way to do that is to consider the church in its infancy. In Acts 2, Luke introduced us to the true church, which was born at Pentecost. What he revealed is the basic divine design for the ordinary church.

> They were continually devoting themselves to the apostles' teaching and to fellowship, to the breaking of bread and to prayer. Everyone kept feeling a sense of awe; and many wonders and signs were taking place through the

> apostles. And all those who had believed were together and had all things in common; and they began selling their property and possessions and were sharing them with all, as anyone might have need. Day by day continuing with one mind in the temple, and breaking bread from house to house, they were taking their meals together with gladness and sincerity of heart, praising God and having favor with all the people. And the Lord was adding to their number day by day those who were being saved. (Acts 2:42–47)

Of course, some will object that the church that was led by the apostles, and where "many wonders and signs were taking place" could not be considered ordinary. But that is the only feature of the church in Acts 2 that differs from the ordinary life of the church through history—one that cannot be replicated because those signs were associated with the apostles.

Leaving aside that one unique detail, the first church was the model for an ordinary church.

ORDINARY ACTIVITIES

The church in Acts 2 was probably not that different from a faithful church today. The people in the church devoted themselves to many of the same activities and attitudes practiced in ordinary churches through history. That is, "They were continually devoting themselves to the apostles' teaching and to fellowship, to the breaking of bread and to prayer" (2:42). Those are the ordinary things that every church should be engaged in.

This is the life of the church. Nothing is in there about entertainment or spectacle. Nothing revivalistic is involved—nothing designed to catapult anyone to some mystical or emotional height. The early church establishes the ordinary activities for every church in every age.

Saved

Verse 42 begins, "They were continually devoting themselves." But who are "they"? Luke referred to the 3,000 souls that were saved at Pentecost (2:41). Combined with those who remained after Christ's ascension, the Acts 2 church was a fairly large congregation—about 3,120 altogether (Acts 1:15). So the first thing we need to recognize about the ordinary church is that though it was large, it was made up of true and baptized believers (2:41). It is regenerate.

Unless a church is composed of the redeemed, it is seriously compromised. Of course, nonbelievers are welcome to come. We're grateful to have them attend and be exposed to the truth of God's Word. But they are not the church. We invite them to come to faith in Christ to become part of the church, but even that depends on God taking the initial action. He is the one who builds His church, and reveals through transformed lives who truly belongs to the body of Christ.

Many churches today design their events to make unbelievers feel like they're the most important people present. They intentionally blur the line, working hard to make unrepentant sinners feel at home in the midst of God's people. They pare down the gospel and tiptoe around difficult or convicting and unpopular biblical subjects to make the unregenerate as comfortable as possible. That inevitably breeds confusion and false conversions. And it opens a pathway for false teaching and worldly corruption to invade the congregation.

Christ warned against that very thing in His letter to the church at Pergamum. "I have a few things against you, because you have there some who hold the teaching of Balaam, who kept teaching Balak to put a stumbling block before the sons of Israel, to eat things sacrificed to idols and to commit acts of immorality. So you also have some who in the same way hold the teaching of the Nicolaitans" (Rev. 2:14–15).

The Lord made it clear that this problem needed to be addressed immediately. "Therefore repent; or else I am coming to you quickly, and I will make war against them with the sword of My mouth" (2:16).

That's a compromised church. They had tolerated idolatry and so blurred the line between regenerate and unregenerate, and were suffering the corrupting consequences and facing judgment from the Lord.

The ordinary church is first and foremost a regenerate people who are in the body of Christ. They are His redeemed—they must be, to be part of His church. That's the critical criterion, and obviously, the church must be saved for it to function as God designed and intended it as His kingdom on earth.

Committed to the Word

Luke pointed out a second fundamental feature in Acts 2:42. "They were continually devoting themselves to the apostles' teaching."

The ordinary church is devoted wholly to the Word of God. The first ordinary church followed obediently the apostles' teaching. Some translations refer to it as "the apostles' doctrine"— a reference to the fact that the apostles were the bearers of divine revelation. Before the completion of the New Testament, the apostles' teaching was authenticated by miracles—which validated them as spokesmen for God (2 Cor. 12:12). These apostles and their associates were the ones who eventually wrote their doctrine as Scripture to pass on to future generations of the church. The Old Testament, along with their teaching, composes the Word of God, the sole revelation from the Holy Spirit to the church. An ordinary church is faithfully committed and wholly submissive to the Bible.

For the true church, biblical truth or doctrine is everything. Sometimes people can be a little skeptical about or intimidated by that word, "doctrine." The Greek word *didachē* just means "teaching." It refers to truth clarified, taught, dispersed, and disseminated. And the doctrine of the apostles conveys the truth from the Lord defining the life of the church of God's redeemed. An ordinary church is completely committed to the renewing of the members' minds through the Word of God.

Christ's final, commissioning words to His disciples were, "Go therefore and make disciples of all the nations, baptizing them in the name of the Father and the Son and the Holy Spirit, teaching them to observe all that I commanded you" (Matt. 28:19–20). The ordinary church was born out of those efforts, and it carries on that work to this day.

Being devoted to the apostles' doctrine meant church wasn't about the cleverness or ingenuity of presentation; it wasn't that the message had been framed around the felt needs of the hearers. It was the content of their teaching. Biblical doctrine is at the heart of the life of the ordinary church.

Fellowship

Luke recorded that the ordinary church was also "devoting themselves . . . to fellowship" (Acts 2:42). The Greek word koinōnia refers to spiritual togetherness—it speaks of the bond between partners or teammates.

The members of the church in Acts 2 were a partnership. They were together. They weren't spectators. They didn't attend part time. They lived out their life in a wonderful, blessed kind of fellowship, illustrated most effectively as the body of Christ (1 Cor. 12:12–27).

An ordinary church is not an event for people to attend and watch. It's not a show people can passively observe from a polite distance. The ordinary church has no bystanders, no viewers or subscribers. It's an intimate fellowship of shared life.

The writer of Hebrews exhorted us, "Let us consider how to stimulate one another to love and good deeds, not forsaking our own assembling together, as is the habit of some, but encouraging one another" (Heb.

10:24–25). These verses imply that we can't encourage one another, or stimulate one another to love and good deeds, if we don't faithfully meet together in fellowship. How else can God's people practice the "one anothers" mentioned here?

Of course, technology simplifies our ability to stay in touch with people today, even over great distances. But no email, text message, or virtual meeting can substitute for the benefits and blessings of time spent together with God's people. If anything, our fellowship would be even sweeter if we could leave all the devices at the door and focus on one another.

Most churches today greatly lack genuine, biblical fellowship. This is one of the features of the church that can't be "microwaved"—you can't suddenly leap to a "whole new level" when other people are involved. Many churches now look more like concerts or stage productions. The crowd files in quietly, sits mostly in the dark with intermediate and vague participation, and then files back out at the end. There might be incidental time for passing conversations with friends, but it offers no intimacy. There's no depth, no sense of shared life or accountability.

True fellowship is one of the essential blessings of the ordinary church. God has given us to one another to sharpen each other, bear each other's burdens, build each other, and stimulate each other to godly love and good deeds.

Cross-Centered

Luke mentioned another feature—one that could easily be mistaken as part of the fellowship he just identified. But I think he had more in mind when he singled out "the breaking of bread" (Acts 2:42).

Christ gave only two ordinances to His church: baptism and the Lord's Table, or communion. Verse 41 tells us, "Those who had received his word were baptized." Here, Luke seemed to indicate that this early church also routinely celebrated the Lord's Table. We know from Paul that shared meals were a common feature of the early church's worship service. Jude referred to them as "love feasts" (2:12). These meals often culminated in the celebration of Christ's sacrificial death on behalf of His people.

The Lord's Table is critical to the life of the church. Jesus designed it and commanded His people to observe it regularly (1 Cor. 11:23–25). It's a solemn reminder of the cost of our sin, and the glories of our Savior. It's a sanctifying, purifying, unifying celebration that draws the body together in love and thanksgiving to Christ. The ordinary church is cross-centered in its worship.

Prayer

Luke mentioned one last feature of the Acts 2 church in verse 42—they were also "devoting themselves . . . to prayer." Praying biblically, the way Jesus taught His disciples to do (Matt. 6:9–13), is a selfless act. Such prayers embrace the kingdom of God and the needs of others. There's no mention of "me" or "I" in the Disciples' Prayer—our needs always take a back seat to others' priorities and problems.

That's a far cry from how many Christians pray today. They approach God as though He were a vending machine or a genie granting wishes. They come with shopping lists and tasks for Him to complete. They're not kneeling before the sovereign God of the universe—they're making demands.

It's easy for us to turn to God in prayer when personal needs and crises arise. Trials, illnesses, and deaths all drive us to prayer. But we're not meant to call on the Lord only in our own hard times. Paul instructed us in First Thessalonians 5:16–18, "Rejoice always; pray without ceasing; in everything give thanks; for this is God's will for you in Christ Jesus."

Prayer isn't meant to be a momentary, isolated part of our lives. We are to be in constant communication with God, bringing all the cares and concerns of His church before Him, along with our praise and thanks. Our entire lives should be communion with God for His people and His glory.

The ordinary church is devoted to prayer, both corporately and individually, living constantly conscious of God's presence and searching out His purposes for its participants.

ORDINARY ATTITUDES

Luke's description didn't end there. Just as he recorded the activities of this blossoming congregation, he also described the attitudes that mark the ordinary church.

Fear of God

In verse 43 he wrote, "Everyone kept feeling a sense of awe." The Greek word is phobos, and it could also be translated as "fear." It's not merely terror, but it's primarily reverence. These believers had a sense that the supernatural had arrived in their midst. And in the case of this church, "Many wonders and signs were taking place through the apostles."

However, the fear of God wasn't limited to the New Testament churches pastored and led by the apostles. Believers should encounter a sense of the divine presence in every church where the Word of God is faithfully exposited, where fellowship and spiritual growth thrive, where the cross is celebrated and sin is dealt with biblically, and where the body is united in prayer. In an ordinary church like that, worship will occur that recognizes God's transcendent presence in power and love.

Genuine worship is not manufactured by feelings manipulated with flashing stage lights and pounding, hypnotic music, or by creating elaborate, bizarre experiences to deceive people into imagining they had an encounter with God. There are charismatic meetings where unsuspecting people are led to participate in a charade—they may shout in gibberish, flail on the floor, and fake miracles for the sake of the show.

The true fear of the Lord "is the beginning of wisdom" (Prov. 9:10). It's not artificial. It has nothing to do with mysticism or emotional experiences. That word "awe" is reserved for times when people's minds are stunned because of some powerful, divine reality. It's the evidence of God revealing His truth, as He illuminates hearts and renews minds. It's the fruit of recognizing and reflecting on God's providence, as His Spirit orchestrates all events for His glory and our good. The ordinary church is where God's people recognize and appreciate His Spirit moving through the truth of Scripture in power to transform lives.

Love

Luke reveals another attitude that marked the church in Acts 2. "All those who had believed were together and had all things in common; and they began selling their property and possessions and were sharing them with all, as anyone might have need" (2:44–45). The church was devoted to one another in love.

Was this communal living, as some propose? No, not at all. When Luke wrote that they "had all things in common," he simply meant that they held whatever they possessed lightly in their hands. If somebody else needed it, they gave it up happily. And when more was was needed, they sold what they had, so they could provide for each other.

Many have tried to argue that this is the start of social justice or some kind of socialism. But that's not at all the correct understanding. It's worth noting that no other record is found in Scripture of such extensive sacrificial sharing in any of the other New Testament churches. This was a situation and a solution unique to the birth of the church in Jerusalem.

That church held many pilgrims—maybe hundreds—who did not go home. There was only one church, and this was it. They had been saved, and they chose to remain with the other believers in the early church at that time. There was nowhere else to go. But who would meet the physical needs of these pilgrim people? How would they get food and shelter? God provided through the loving and generous sacrifice of their fellow believers. The Lord was growing this body of believers together in the grace and knowledge of His Word, and they were happy to surrender anything to keep their congregation together.

The ordinary church gives faithfully and generously in love to support the needs of His people.

Unity

Luke continued in verse 46, "Day by day continuing with one mind in the temple, and breaking bread from house to house, they were taking their meals together." They enjoyed blessed unity in the Lord. Their lives were knit together by common spiritual life, shared in their worship and service as they gathered daily together.

The life of this church was not isolated to one day a week. They weren't strangers who gathered together for a few hours and then went their separate ways. They didn't only show up when it was convenient or when it fit into the rest of their schedule. The church was the daily center of their lives; everything else revolved around their fellowship together.

Do you have that experience with the people at your church? Are they relegated to one day and specific events? Or is the church the center of your world? You have more in common with other believers than you do with your coworkers, your neighbors, and even your unbelieving family members. Do you love God's people and long to be with them? The ordinary church is united in love and fellowship.

Joy

We find another attitude revealed at the end of verse 46. Luke wrote that they engaged in the unity of fellowship "with gladness and sincerity of heart." Their unity wasn't just marked by love, but also by joy. They were genuinely glad to be together, even as they sacrificed to provide for each other.

Real joy is another rare commodity in many churches today. Most have petty disputes and animosities constantly brewing under the surface; others don't bother to keep it a secret. But conflict is antithetical to God's design for His church. Believers should be the least-easily-offended people in the world, and the quickest to forgive.

We should contend earnestly for the truth (Jude 3), and we should be on the lookout for wolves (Acts 20:29), but the true church should be marked by harmony, single-mindedness, and joy (Phil. 1:27).

Consider for a moment how your general attitude and perspective affects your testimony. Are you often anxious or angry? Are you dour or stoic? Are you a complainer? Or is your life marked by the joy of the Lord? The people in your life pay attention to these things, and everything in your life—including your attitude—should adorn the gospel and consequently the testimony of your church.

The ordinary church is known for the joy of its people.

Praise

Luke identified a final attitude that marked the church in Acts 2:47 with the simple phrase, "praising God." The church had an undivided focus on worship. This was not the human-centered worship that's so popular today. They weren't hearing sermons about how God wanted to fulfill their hopes and dreams. They weren't singing songs more focused on themselves than their Savior.

God's people exist to praise and glorify His name. We worship Him as Christ commanded, "in spirit and truth" (John 4:23). We recite His glorious attributes and recount His great works. We "worship in the Spirit of God and glory in Christ Jesus and put no confidence in the flesh" (Phil. 3:3). Nothing is performative about it. We render "a sacrifice of praise to God, that is, the fruit of lips that give thanks to His name" (Heb. 13:15). And it's not isolated to a few hours of corporate worship every week. We continually submit ourselves in obedience, as Paul instructed: "Present your bodies a living and holy sacrifice, acceptable to God, which is your spiritual service of worship" (Rom. 12:1).

The ordinary church worships, focusing on the holy pleasure of the Lord of the church, not the carnal feelings of its people.

Ordinary Effects

The church in Acts 2 was an ordinary church. It wasn't flashy, extreme, or over the top. Nothing about the church was designed to grab the attention or win the approval of the culture.

And Luke briefly pointed out the effect this ordinary church had in the first-century world. He commented first that they had "favor with all the people" (Acts 2:47). The ordinary church is a common grace to the surrounding community.

The COVID–19 lockdowns showed how valuable the church is in the world and the disastrous effect of shutting it down. As I mentioned before, in our area, liquor stores and marijuana dispensaries were allowed to stay open—they were considered essential—while the city and state government kept the churches closed.

High-ranking members of law enforcement and other members of the local government reached out to us, expressing their desire for us to remain open. They could see the degrading effects of removing the church's influence from the culture—the hopelessness and depression that took hold of the culture in those days. I know many pastors who received similar encouragement from their local leaders.

It's more than just the collective good, however; the world sees what goes on in our midst. They recognize our love, unity, and joy. They can see that a supernatural transformation is occurring in our churches. All this is the fulfillment of Christ's command in the Sermon on the Mount, "Let your light shine before men in such a way that they may see your good works, and glorify your Father who is in heaven" (Matt. 5:16).

This ordinary church experienced an extraordinary blessing. Luke concluded with this: "And the Lord was adding to their number day by day those who were being saved" (Acts 2:47). The Lord builds His church (more on that in the next chapter). He blessed their faithfulness by drawing more people to His kingdom.

The Lord didn't ask His church to be radical, extreme, alternative, revolutionary, or any other adjective. He asks us to follow the ordinary means of grace and to be faithful to His Word and His Spirit. He will take care of the extraordinary part. He honors the slow, steady, consistent, faithful loyalty to Christ; He blesses obedience, submission to His truth, and holy worship.

And through these ordinary means, the ordinary church will, by the power of God, have an extraordinary impact.

Study Questions:

1. Do you find that you lack respect for the "ordinary"? If yes, why do you think that is?

2. What activities of the church in Acts 2 do we still practice today?

3. What does it mean to "fear" God? How should the "fear of the Lord" influence the way we worship?

4. How can you ensure that prayer doesn't become something you only do in times of crisis?

5. What is the harm in designing church programs and practices to appeal to unbelievers?

6. Explain in your own words how "doctrine is everything" for the true church.

2

The Church and Election

I RECENTLY DID AN Internet search on the phrase "heaven on earth"—I wanted to see how others might identify that concept. It turns out that Heaven on Earth is located less than three miles from Grace Community Church. With a few clicks, I found out a little more about the establishment. Their mission statement was particularly interesting: "The mission of Heaven on Earth Society for Animals is to transform the lives of homeless cats through rescue, sanctuary, and new beginnings." It identified itself as a "cage-free, no-kill facility." That's a pretty grandiose title to self-apply for simply not killing stray cats.

The truth of the matter is that the church is heaven on earth. The church of God, gathered and composed of those who have been called by Him to have faith in the Lord Jesus Christ, constitutes His kingdom in the world. In that sense, the church is as close to heaven as you can get here on earth.

We need to understand that singular identity of the church. So let's begin with a biblical definition. In the opening words of his epistle to the believers in Corinth, Paul gave us a powerful explanation. He wrote, "To the church of God which is at Corinth, to those who have been sanctified in Christ Jesus, saints by calling, with all who in every place call on the name of our Lord Jesus Christ, their Lord and ours" (1 Cor. 1:2).

The church is, first of all, the church of God. It belongs to Him because He purchased it. It is the body of those who have been sanctified, set apart from sin because they are now in Christ. They are "saints by calling"—that is, they are saints because God ordained to save them and called them out of the darkness of sin and spiritual death. And they are marked as such "in every place" as those who confess Jesus as Lord. That's the church.

A few verses later, Paul provided us with the divine perspective. First Corinthians 1:9 says, "God is faithful, through whom you were called into fellowship with His Son, Jesus Christ our Lord."

Faithful to do what? Paul spelled that out in verse 8: to "confirm you to the end, blameless in the day of our Lord Jesus Christ." The church of Jesus Christ, then, are those who belong to God, purchased by Him, who have been separated from sin and judgment by the work of Christ and faith in Him, who have been called as saints, who confess Jesus as Lord, who have been given the promise that this salvation is permanent. And one day they will be gathered together, blameless in the presence of the Lord Jesus Christ, according to God, who will faithfully fulfill all those promises.

The church is not a building. It's not an institution of religion. It's not an ethical organization or a sociopolitical association. The church is the assembly of those chosen and called by God, redeemed by Christ, and secured by the Holy Spirit to final glory. It is the body of redeemed sinners called out of darkness into eternal light.

We find the same defining characteristics throughout the pages of Scripture. Colossians 1:13–14 says, "For He rescued us from the domain of darkness, and transferred us to the kingdom of His beloved Son, in whom we have redemption, the forgiveness of sins."

We were helpless and hopeless, slaves in Satan's domain, marked by sin and death. But we have been transferred by the power of God into the kingdom of His Son, our Savior. Our sins have been forgiven—we've been rescued and redeemed.

The author of Hebrews referred to the church as "the general assembly . . . of the firstborn"—that is, Christ—"who are enrolled in heaven" (Heb. 12:23). We belong to the heavenly kingdom, and Christ is our King. Paul put it simply in Philippians 3:20, "Our citizenship is in heaven."

Our Father is in heaven, our Savior is in heaven, our fellow saints are in heaven—and so are we already, in terms of our citizenship, while we look forward to our future glorification. Or as Paul explained, "Our citizenship is in heaven, from which also we eagerly wait for a Savior, the Lord Jesus Christ; who will transform the body of our humble state into conformity with the body of His glory, by the exertion of the power that He has even to subject all things to Himself" (3:20–21). We are already spiritual citizens of heaven, and one day we will be physically glorified and taken there through the power of Christ.

A Foretaste of Heaven

All of that points to the fact that the church on earth is to be a foretaste of heaven. Although it is imperfect, the church is the only place where you could honestly say heaven comes down to earth, because the activities of heaven are reflected in the life of the church.

In the church, God's people desire to worship Him. God's people love Him. They submit to His moral will as expressed in Scripture and seek to obey Him out of devotion. All the activities of the church are a taste of what will be perfected in heaven.

Take worship, for example. In the church, believers continually offer adoration to God. Hebrews 13:15 referred to it as "a sacrifice of praise to God, that is, the fruit of lips that give thanks to His name." Such expressions of worship are exactly what heaven is doing continually. According to Revelation 4:8, "Day and night they do not cease to say, 'Holy, holy, holy is the Lord God, the Almighty, who was and who is and who is to come.'" For all eternity, along with the holy angels, the citizens of heaven will exalt the Lord.

Our submission to God is likewise a faint echo of heaven in the church. We bring heaven down, in a sense, fulfilling the words the Lord taught His church to pray in Matthew 6:10, "Your will be done, on earth as it is in heaven." That can only happen in one place—the church. While we have not yet been perfected, we provide a glimpse of virtue and righteousness in ways that are notably different from the world around us. The church is to be set apart from the immorality, idolatry, and impurity that dominate this fallen earth. And although we cannot manifest the perfect holiness and purity of heaven, we are nonetheless called to be holy and pure in ways that characterize heaven for the watching world.

Christian fellowship is another example. In the church, we enjoy rich, deep fellowship with other believers. We might not share personal interests or life experiences, but the most important thing about us—our shared love for Christ—unites us in a transcendent way. The love and fellowship shared among mature believers is the richest of all possible human relations because it is a taste of what's to come in heaven. But it is only a preview, as we will all be perfectly united in Christ into an everlasting fellowship that we can't fully comprehend on this side of heaven.

Our Christ-centered worship, our submission to God's will in pursuing holiness, and our flourishing fellowship with other believers—those are just some of the ways the church on earth foreshadows the glories of heaven. It's strange to think about how many churches today are trying to be as much like the world as possible, when that defies the entire purpose of the church's existence.

Instead, God's people must follow Paul's charge to the Colossians.

> If you have been raised up with Christ, keep seeking the things above, where Christ is, seated at the right hand of God. Set your mind on the things above, not on the things that are on earth. For you have died and your life is hidden with Christ in God. When Christ, who is our life, is revealed, then you also will be revealed with Him in glory. (3:1–4)

In the meantime, we each must "consider the members of your earthly body as dead to immorality, impurity, passion, evil desire, and greed, which amounts to idolatry" (3:5), because these things bring about God's wrath (3:6). We have been transformed and set free from our former way of life and the bondage of sin and death. We have been made citizens of heaven, and we are to act like it. That's why we need to look at the church as heaven on earth. And it's why whatever is true of heaven should also, in some measure, be manifestly true of the redeemed church.

Foundational Doctrines

I have found an incredible joy in giving my life to the ministry of one church for over half a century. I've loved every moment of it, even the trying times, because I love the church. But make no mistake—it's not my church. I've been granted a stewardship over something that doesn't belong to me. It's not subject to my preferences or shaped by my sensibilities. It's God's church—His alone. I'm just a steward. And stewards are required to be faithful, because we will give an account for how we have cared for the little bit of heaven on earth assigned to us (1 Cor. 4:2–4).

That is why we need to understand what the King has said about His kingdom. First Timothy 3:15 refers to the church as "the pillar and ground of the truth" (NKJV). The English Standard Version translates it as "pillar and buttress," while the New American Standard renders it as "pillar and support," but each iteration points to the same illustration.

Paul was writing to Timothy, who was in Ephesus at the time. The city was also home to the temple of Diana, which was said to be the most astonishing of all the Seven Wonders of the Ancient World. It was held up by 127 pillars, each one carved out of marble and overlaid with gold.

But this awe-inspiring edifice was nothing more than a gilded tomb—a monument to Satan and spiritual death. Its foundation was false religion and immoral paganism. It was a temple to lies. By contrast, Paul reminded Timothy that the church is to be the pillar and ground, or the buttress of the truth.

For the true, redeemed church, everything is about the truth. It sets the biblical foundation for all our understanding of who we are and how we're meant to live. You cannot understand the church according to sociology, psychology, or some other means of personal interpretation. To truly understand the church, you have to understand the revelation of God concerning the doctrine that defines the church.

Specifically, we need to look at five foundational doctrines that shape our biblical understanding of the church. You could call them the five pillars of the redeemed church. And the first is God's work in election.

Our Sovereign God

Any study of God's electing work needs to begin with understanding His role as sovereign over all of creation. Consider how He describes those unique qualities through the prophet Isaiah.

> Thus says the Lord, the King of Israel and his Redeemer, the Lord of hosts: "I am the first and I am the last, and there is no God besides Me. Who is like Me? Let him proclaim and declare it; yes, let him recount it to Me in order, from the time that I established the ancient nation. And let them declare to them the things that are coming and the events that are going to take place. Do not tremble and do not be afraid; have I not long since announced it to you and declared it? And you are My witnesses. Is there any God besides Me, or is there any other Rock? I know of none." (Isa. 44:6–8)

God is the lone sovereign over His creation. He is the first and the last—He predates any rivals to His authority, and He will outlast any pretenders to His throne. No one else can describe how creation came into being because there is only one Creator. And no one else can tell us what's to come in the future, because there is only one Author of history. All events, from the dawn of creation to the end of time, unfold according to His sovereign plan. The triune God alone determines all things. No one is above Him.

He makes the same point again a few chapters later.

> Remember this, and be assured; recall it to mind, you transgressors. Remember the former things long past, For I am God, and there is no other; I am God, and there is no one like Me, declaring the end from the beginning, and from ancient times things which have not been done, saying, "My purpose will be established, and I will accomplish all My good pleasure." (Isa. 46:8–10)

God is sovereign over all people and events. History is His story. He wrote the ending at the beginning, along with everything in between. He orchestrates everything and everyone through His providence to bring about His plan of redemption, for our good and His glory.

That includes the building of His church.

The Church Is Built by the Lord

Matthew's Gospel provides us with the defining statement on this. Replying to Peter's affirmation of His divinity, Jesus declared, "I will build My church; and the gates of Hades will not overpower it" (Matt. 16:18).

The faithful, immutable, omnipotent, sovereign Lord of heaven, whose Word cannot return void but always accomplishes what He says, whose purposes always come to pass, whose will is always fulfilled, and whose plan is both invincible and unshakable—He is the One who will build His church, and no power on earth or in hell can prevail against it.

Christ specifically used "the gates of Hades" as an opposing force to His work. He was using a familiar Jewish expression. Hades was the place of the dead, and the gates of Hades were a reference to the entrance that ushered souls in—that is, death itself. What He was really identifying here was the primary weapon in Satan's arsenal. Hebrews 2 declares that the devil holds the power of death, and by it, keeps men in the bondage of fear throughout their lives (2:14–15). But even the power of death that takes the life of saints cannot keep the Lord from building His church.

This is a triumphant promise from the Lord. The most powerful and fearsome weapon that Satan wields under the sovereignty of God is utterly impotent to stop the church. It takes God's people into eternity, but it cannot thwart His work or the fulfillment of His design for His church.

The reason for that invincibility resides in the nature of the church. It is not a human organization. It doesn't belong to us. It's not built by the cleverness or strategies of men; it doesn't depend on our tactics or ingenuity. Christ is unequivocal—it is His church, and He alone is building it. And as a result, nothing will stop it.

A reporter who asked me about my desire to build the church may have been surprised when I replied, "I have no desire to build the church. Jesus said He would build the church, and I don't want to compete with Him."

Moreover, I have no ability to build the church in the first place. I have no power to add to the kingdom. The best of my sermons can't awaken the dead or give sight to the blind. Only God can transform the sinner's heart and grant spiritual life. I can throw seed, but I can't change the soil.

The church is God's church. It belongs to Him, and it's the only institution in the world that He is building. Everything else is destined for the fire of His judgment, whether it's the material creation that goes out of existence or the unregenerate person who will end up in the eternal punishment of hell.

Heaven awaits only one entity: the assembly of the redeemed. Ultimately, the Lord will blend His church together with the Old Testament saints to compose the final bride of Christ. Until then, the work of building His church continues until it is complete.

Our Role in the Lord's Work

The only questions for us, then, are by what means is He building it, and how do we serve Him in the process?

The apostle Paul provided us with an answer in Titus 1. As he opened this marvelous epistle, Paul identified himself as both "a bond-servant of God and an apostle of Jesus Christ" (1:1). First of all, he was a slave of God. And the very character of that slavery—or the specific task that he bore—was to serve as an apostle on behalf of Jesus Christ. He was God's slave who was given the duty of being a messenger for Christ; specifically "for the faith of those chosen of God and the knowledge of the truth with is according to godliness, in the hope of eternal life, which God, who cannot lie, promised long ages ago" (1:1–2).

Those two verses essentially define for us the nature of all biblical ministry. Paul, as a slave of God and a chosen messenger of Jesus Christ, was sent to accomplish three things. The first was a ministry of evangelism, which he described in the words, "For the faith of those chosen of God."

He was given the task of preaching the gospel so that the elect would hear it and believe. Paul recognized that he had no power to save sinners. But he understood that God had chosen whom He would save before the foundations of the world, and Paul preached the gospel so that the chosen could understand it and exercise the gift of faith that God bestowed on them.

The apostle understood that his initial role in God's work was to preach the gospel. He illustrated the importance of the evangelistic aspect of his ministry in his epistle to the Romans. "How then will they call on Him in whom they have not believed? How will they believe in Him whom they have not heard? And how will they hear without a preacher?" (Rom. 10:14).

Paul's job was to bring people to the point of salvation, or justification, through the preaching of the gospel. As he put it, "Faith comes from hearing, and hearing by the word of Christ" (10:17).

He identified a second crucial aspect of his ministry in Titus 1:1, which he described as "the knowledge of the truth which is according to godliness." This is the ministry of edification. Beyond bringing the truth of the gospel, he wanted also to bring to God's chosen people the fullness of the knowledge of the truth so that they might live godly lives. Just as he was committed to seeing God's people justified by the truth (1 Pet. 1:22–25), he also wanted to see them sanctified by the truth (John 17:17).

Finally, Paul described the third aspect of biblical ministry in the opening words of verse 2, "In the hope of eternal life." We could call this the ministry of encouragement—he was pointing believers to the hope of heaven and their future glorification as motivation to persevere through their pilgrimage and service to their Lord in this hostile, wicked world.

That captures God's church-building work—to save, sanctify, and glorify those whom He chose in eternity past. That is the great, unfolding, comprehensive redemptive purpose of God. And in His sovereign plan, He has given us a part to play through proclaiming His Word—for the evangelism, edification, and consolation of His chosen people.

A Promise from Eternity Past

There's more. Paul continued in Titus 1:2, "Which God, who cannot lie, promised long ages ago," or as the original language says, "Before time began."

This tells us that in eternity past, before anything or anyone had been created or time began, God determined to start and complete His redemptive plan. People were chosen. Their names were written down that they might be brought to faith, to godliness, and to glory. God promised all this before time began.

To whom did God make this promise? It wasn't to angels. Our best understanding regarding the angels is that they were created sometime just before the creation of the rest of the universe. So in the pre-creation state, who was there for God to make any promises to?

We find some helpful insight in Second Timothy 1:8–9. Verse 8 ends with a reference to God, making Him the antecedent and the one Paul described in verse 9—that is, God, "who has saved us and called us with a holy calling, not according to our works, but according to His own purpose and grace which was granted us in Christ Jesus from all eternity."

Here again we see the same Greek phrase that means, "Before time began." This whole covenant—God's complete plan of redemption, laid down in eternity past to choose, save, sanctify, and glorify a people for Himself—was a pledge made by the Father and the Son. The promise made before time began was from God to the Lord Jesus Christ.

This is a staggering reality. In the mystery of the Trinity, its members share an indescribable and inexplicable love. Jesus alluded to it in His high-priestly prayer when He asked the Father to love His own the way He loved the Son and asked that they might share in the mutual love between the Son and the Father. That love must find its expression. And the Father, in a demonstration of this indescribable, supernatural, perfect love, expressed to the Son a desire to manifest that love in a massive way.

Hebrews 13:20 refers to this as "the eternal covenant." The Father has promised the Son a redeemed humanity—justified, sanctified, and glorified to magnify and reflect His glory for all eternity, as an expression of His love.

This is a staggering reality, and it becomes even more profound when we look at John 6. In verse 37, Jesus said, "All that the Father gives Me will come to Me."

There, in just a few words, is the invincibility of the church. Every individual ever redeemed, every person granted the gift of faith, everyone ever forgiven and justified before God by His grace is a love gift from the Father to the Son. You didn't choose to save yourself—no one did. Every person God chose to save in eternity past was chosen for the express purpose of glorifying, praising, honoring, and worshipping the Son forever and ever.

That is the Father's expression of love to the Son—in the most wonderful way He could do it. True, He created the angels, and the holy ones worship the Son, as well. But the church is unique because the members of it are redeemed from sin and death and raised to heaven as the Bride of Christ to glorify Him forever.

Christ continued in verse 37, "And the one who comes to Me I will certainly not cast out." Of course, the Son won't turn down a love gift from the Father. He would no more reject one the Father has given Him as a love gift than to reject the Father He loved perfectly.

In fact, in verse 38, Jesus explained that He had a crucial part in the fulfillment of the Father's promise. He said, "I have come down from heaven, not to do My own will, but the will of Him who sent Me." That doesn't mean Christ was unwilling or reluctant in any way. It only means that He came willingly to fulfill His Father's will for Him. He was saying He accomplished the work that was necessary to provide the atoning sacrifice so that the elect could be redeemed. He alone could serve as the perfect sacrifice for His people. He was the only One who could be their Savior.

"This is the will of Him who sent Me, that of all that He has given Me I lose nothing, but raise it up on the last day. For this is the will of My Father, that everyone who beholds the Son and believes in Him will have eternal life, and I Myself will raise him up on the last day" (John 6:39–40).

Again, we face the invincibility of God's redeeming purpose. All His chosen people will ultimately be glorified, not only because God said so but also because Jesus will make it so. We're an untouchable, imperishable love gift within the Trinity. We're caught up in something monumental and transcendent. It's as though our individual salvation is somewhat incidental to the real issue at hand, which is to express love between the Father and the Son. You and I are not the focus—we're just the gift.

It is true that God loves sinners. He does, indeed, love the world, but He loves His own people in an eternal and unique way. John 13:1 explains that Christ "loved His own who were in the world, He loved them to the end."

But that love is only an intermediary love. He loves believers so that He might express that greatest of all blessings on them as the bride for His Son. And in eternity, we will serve, honor, and glorify the Son—and one more thing: we will be made like Him. In the words of Romans 8:29, "For those whom He foreknew, He also predestined to *become* conformed to the image of His Son, so that He would be the firstborn among many brethren."

As much as redeemed and glorified humanity can be like incarnate deity, we will be like Christ, so that He will be the firstborn (Gk., *prōtotokos*), or the premier one "among many brethren." Imitation is the supreme compliment, and the Father will glorify believers by conforming them to the image of the Son.

We won't *be* God; we don't become deities. We will be a glorified humanity that reflects the glory of the One who saved us. We will possess His holiness, and we will be His all-glorious bride. And "then comes the end, when [Christ] hands over the kingdom to the God and Father" (1 Cor. 15:24), and reciprocates the love gift to the Father, "so that God may be all in all" (15:28). All of it is a divine work, to fulfill God's promise in eternity past.

In Romans 8, Paul concluded, as we should, that God's work of building His church would not be hindered or impeded in any way. In verse 31 he wrote, "What then shall we say to these things? If God is for us, who is against us?" The work of building the church doesn't rise and fall with any man.

It's God's work. He will build the host of His people, and nothing can stand against His eternal redemptive plan.

Study Questions:

1. Explain in your own words how the church is "heaven on earth."
2. What does it mean to say, "Our citizenship is in heaven"? How does that statement affect the way you live?
3. Why do we have confidence that the church is invincible?
4. What promise was made between God the Father and God the Son before creation? What part do you play in the fulfillment of that promise?
5. Since God alone is sovereign over salvation and the growth of His church, why do we still evangelize?

3

The Church and Identification

THIS WORLD IS NOT our home. Scripture clearly shows that we are "aliens and strangers" on this earth (1 Pet. 2:11). As we already discussed, "our citizenship is in heaven" (Phil. 3:20).

If you're a believer in the Lord Jesus Christ, you are a citizen of the kingdom of God. That means your home is in heaven. Your spiritual family of glorified saints is in heaven, too—what the author of Hebrews refers to as "the spirits of the righteous made perfect" (Heb. 12:23).

Of course, your King is in heaven, along with the eternal inheritance He has prepared for you (1 Pet. 1:3–5). And according to Christ, your heart should already be there. "Do not store up for yourselves treasures on earth, where moth and rust destroy, and where thieves break in and steal. But store up for yourselves treasures in heaven, where neither moth nor rust destroys, and where thieves do not break in or steal; for where your treasure is, there your heart will be also" (Matt. 6:19–21). Following those instructions should curtail our affections for this fleeting life. It should fix our eyes on His heavenly kingdom (Col. 3:1) and tether our allegiance to Him alone.

God's people need to do everything they can to loosen ties with this world and live as citizens of heaven. As we consider the doctrinal pillars that uphold the redeemed church, we must next give attention to the issue of identification.

Heaven's Colony

As Peter puts it, believers "are A CHOSEN RACE, A royal PRIESTHOOD, A HOLY NATION, A PEOPLE FOR *God's* OWN POSSESSION . . . for you once were not a people, but now you are THE PEOPLE OF GOD" (1 Pet. 2:9–10). We have been adopted into God's eternal family, and our entire identity is bound up in Him. We are His children.

In a sense, we should think of the church as a colony of heaven. Colonization on a national level has taken on a pejorative connotation in recent years, but throughout much of world history, it was one of the primary ways kingdoms and cultures expanded their progress for the advance of society. When the ruler of a particular nation wanted to increase the accomplishments of his society, he would plant a colony and establish a foothold somewhere else around the globe, often in a faraway place.

This was also a means to laying claim to another part of the world—both its people and its resources—by making it part of his larger kingdom. It meant that the men and women of the colony and the resources were available to the authority of the colonizing nation, subject to the laws of his kingdom, and, beneficiaries of the rights, privileges, and blessings of citizenship. Ideally it was for mutual benefit. Thirteen such colonies became the United States of America, and many other countries today similarly got their start as colonies of other nations.

In some of the same ways, the church is a colony of heaven. Our King is in heaven and rules over us from there. His law is there, but it also extends to His colony on earth, and we, from the heart, obey it. His power and presence are in heaven, but also manifest in His people on earth through the indwelling of the Holy Spirit. We are the outpost of the culture of heaven. We are to reflect our King—to adhere to His holy law and to exemplify His character in His kingdom on earth.

Tragically, many churches have lost sight of that identity and are more concerned about being like the world rather than to be heavenly. They flout our King's righteous law, and they manipulate His Word to suit their priorities and preferences. Rather than living distinctly separate from the world and devoted to their King, they attempt to court the world's approval through appeasement and entertainment. In short, they are disloyal to their King.

But the will of our sovereign is not difficult to know. We're not waiting on voices from heaven or opinions from earth to provide us with direction; His will is revealed to us in His Word. As Paul said, "We have the mind of Christ" (1 Cor. 2:16). We know what our King wills and what He desires of us—specifically that the "gospel of the kingdom shall be preached in the whole world as a testimony to all the nations" (Matt. 24:14). The good news concerning our King and His kingdom, along with all its duties and blessings, is to be honored and proclaimed faithfully.

We are the messengers who bring the good news of Christ and the forgiveness of sins to a lost and dying world. We are the heralds of His truth. We're

His ambassadors in a corrupt and hostile land, pleading with those around us to enter His kingdom through repentance and faith while there is still time.

A Precious Commodity

The Word of God has much more to say about the depth and riches of our new identity in Christ.

To begin with, Scripture tells us that the church is the most precious reality on earth. To be clear, we're not precious to the world. They don't like or understand us. Often, they resent us because our very existence is a rebuke to their wickedness. Our message stings their consciences.

In the case of the true church, popularity doesn't come with value. The true church is the most precious reality on earth. How do I know that? Because of the immense cost that was paid for us as the church. Christ paid the highest imaginable price to redeem us to Himself. In the words of First Peter 1:18–19, "You were not redeemed with perishable things like silver or gold from your futile way of life . . . but with precious blood, as of a lamb unblemished and spotless, *the blood* of Christ."

The price paid for us was greater than any price ever paid for anything. We are "the church of God which He purchased with His own blood" (Acts 20:28). Paul reminded the Corinthians, "You have been bought with a price" (1 Cor. 6:20)—one far higher than we can even conceive.

How valuable is the church? It's so precious that the Son was willing to come to die as the price required for the Father's love gift to become a reality.

One verse defines how valuable the church is to God. Extolling the sacrifice of our Savior, Paul wrote, "For you know the grace of our Lord Jesus Christ, that though He was rich, yet for your sake He became poor, so that you through His poverty might become rich" (2 Cor. 8:9).

Many people have twisted the meaning of that verse; some try to equate the gospel with financial poverty, while others use it to legitimize their own vast wealth. But that verse has absolutely nothing to do with Christ's economic circumstances—or your own.

Paul was not talking about earthly riches or material goods. He was saying that the pre-incarnate Son of God was rich in all the same ways that God is rich. He was rich in glory and majesty. That means the phrase "yet for your sake He became poor" wasn't talking about Jesus' material poverty either. Paul was saying that our Lord and Savior, possessor of all divine glory, humbled Himself by becoming a man. It's the poverty of being a human in relation to the unsurpassed riches of being God.

It's important to understand that Christ's financial situation had nothing to do with His redemptive work. It wouldn't have mattered whether He were the poorest man in town or the richest—His economic status was in no way meritorious or material to His saving work.

Rather, Paul was pointing our attention to the poverty the Lord experienced in the sense that, by virtue of His incarnation and behind the veil of His humanity, He did not always fully express His glory and majesty. The apostle stated the reality of the incarnation in his epistle to the Philippians.

> Have this attitude in yourselves which was also in Christ Jesus, who, although He existed in the form of God, did not regard equality with God a thing to be grasped, but emptied Himself, taking the form of a bond-servant, *and* being made in the likeness of men. Being found in appearance as a man, He humbled Himself by becoming obedient to the point of death, even death on a cross. (Phil. 2:5–8)

The infinitely powerful Creator and Sustainer of our entire universe chose to take on the frailties and limitations of humanity. The One who designed every plant and animal, who spoke the sun and moon into existence and divided day from night, took on a body that required food and sleep. A body that would be bruised and beaten, lacerated with whips and spat on, and was ultimately nailed to a cross to endure the agonies and public humiliations of crucifixion. And from the depths of this poverty and His alienation from the Father, He would cry out, "MY GOD, MY GOD, WHY HAVE YOU FORSAKEN ME?" (Matt. 27:46).

That's the kind of poverty Paul had in mind. And that's the incalculable cost Christ paid to rescue us from the slavery of sin.

Why? "So that you through His poverty might become rich" (2 Cor. 8:9). Christ endured the humiliations of the incarnation so that we could be joint heirs with Him in eternity (Rom. 8:17). He became poor by taking on the poverty of humanity, so that you might gain heaven's riches.

IMPUTATION AND IDENTITY

When considering Christ's condescension and the price He paid on our behalf, there is perhaps no more staggering description than the one Paul provided in Second Corinthians 5:21. The apostle wrote, "He made Him who knew no sin"—and that's not hard to interpret. Only one person could be described like that. In the whole history of creation, only one man qualifies for that designation—the Lord Jesus Christ.

Paul explains that God made Jesus, the sinless one, "*to be* sin on our behalf." That's how poor He became. To fulfill God's plan to redeem His church, Christ not only set aside the riches and majesty of heaven, but He was made "*to be* sin on our behalf."

In what way did Christ become sin? Many false teachers will tell you this verse means Jesus actually became a sinner. They even say that He had to go to hell for three days to pay the penalty for His sins.

That's blasphemy. Jesus never sinned—He lived a perfect life, fulfilling all righteousness (Matt. 3:15). He certainly didn't become a sinner on the cross. He was never guilty of any sin (Heb. 7:26). Hanging on the cross, He was completely innocent. No sin could be put to His account. He was still fully God, and didn't even have the capacity to sin—if He had, He would have ceased to be God. It simply wasn't possible. In no sense did the Lord Jesus ever become a sinner.

So then what happened? What was Paul saying here?

He was using simple language to unpack a complex, powerful truth for us—a doctrine that theologians refer to as *imputation*. While Jesus never committed a sin Himself, God treated Him as if He had personally committed every sin of every person who would ever be saved. All our sin was imputed to Him and He bore its punishment.

It's difficult to really grasp that thought. The enormous weight of just one person's life of sin is hard enough to comprehend on its own. But Christ bore the punishment for every sin committed by every person who would ever believe. God heaped the full fury of His just wrath on His Son as if He were guilty of all of it, when the fact is He was guilty of none of it. And the punishment for all that sin was fully expiated, so that it could never be held against those who believe.

No sin will go unpunished. All of God's righteous wrath will be expressed and every penalty for sin will be meted out. The fierce cost of every sin will be paid—either in the inextinguishable fires of hell or on the cross.

And only Christ could have paid that price. He, alone, could be our suitable sacrifice. Only an infinite person could withstand the infinite penalty our sin demands. He endured the fullness of the wrath of that which rightly belonged to us—an exponential eternity of torment and separation from God, covering the incalculable cost for all of God's elect—in a matter of just a few hours.

There was no remainder; no balance left unpaid. He completely covered the collective cost of a debt we could never individually pay. Outside of the cross, God's judgment against sin is unending—it won't ever be exhausted. In Christ, God's judgment was fully completed.

But that's only the first half of imputation—there's a second aspect to this great exchange. Paul wrote, "He made Him who knew no sin to be sin on our behalf, so that we might become the righteousness of God in Him" (2 Cor. 5:21). Jesus was not a sinner on the cross, and we're not righteous.

God's people can't afford to pretend that we're sinless. In fact, if we truly understand the ongoing war with our sinful flesh, we have to echo the mournful cry of Paul in Romans 7: "For I know that nothing good dwells in me, that is, in my flesh; for the willing is present in me, but the doing of the good is not. For the good that I want, I do not do, but I practice the very evil that I do not want. . . . Wretched man that I am! Who will set me free from the body of this death?" (7:18–19, 24). You and I aren't any more righteous than Jesus was sinful.

But in this lies the awe-striking beauty of imputation. Just as He imputed our sin to Christ, He imputes Christ's righteousness to us. On the cross, God treated Jesus as if He had lived your life of sin, so that forever He could treat you as if you had lived Christ's perfect life of righteousness. The perfect and holy Son of God was cloaked in the filthy rags of our sin so that we can be draped in the spotless robes of His righteousness.

That's imputation—perhaps the fullest and best expression of God's grace to His elect. We are credited with a righteousness we could never achieve on our own. Our spiritual account isn't merely zeroed out. We've been granted the infinite credit of our Savior's life of perfect holiness. And for eternity, when our heavenly Father looks at us, He will see only the perfect, righteous life of His Son.

That's the incredible, incalculable price Christ paid for us—one that covers our penalty and grants us the credit of His life before our Judge. And that infinite price makes the church the most precious reality on earth.

One with Christ

We need to consider one more aspect of the true church's identity. If you're a believer, Christ's righteousness has been imputed to you, and the efficacy of both His righteous death and His righteous life been credited to your account. But it doesn't end there—Christ Himself has taken up residence in you.

Believers are so inseparably connected to Christ that Paul could write, "I have been crucified with Christ; and it is no longer I who live, but Christ lives in me; and the *life* which I now live in the flesh I live by faith in the Son of God, who loved me and gave Himself up for me" (Gal. 2:20).

What an amazing statement—"It is no longer I who live, but Christ lives in me." God's people need to cultivate that mindset. The Lord is not remote or withdrawn. He is actively involved, living within us and empowering us for the work of His kingdom.

We are one with Christ. Our bodies are the temple of His Holy Spirit (1 Cor. 6:19), who is constantly working within us to sanctify us, growing us in the likeness of Lord and Savior. Or as Paul put it just a few verses earlier, "The one who joins himself to the Lord is one spirit *with Him*" (6:17).

That has massive implications for the church. When I look out at our congregation, I realize I'm not just dealing with people—I'm dealing with Christ. This reality should inform our stewardship of one another. It should define and direct the way we interact with and treat each other. Christ Himself speaks to that very issue in Matthew 18.

Here, in what is essentially a primitive chapter discussing the life of the church, are some vital truths from the Lord of the church. Verse 1 says, "The disciples came to Jesus and said, 'Who then is greatest in the kingdom of heaven?'"

This seems to have been a continual debate among the disciples, especially early in their time with Christ. They constantly jockeyed for position among one another, and whenever the opportunity presented itself, they asked Jesus to arbitrate their petty disputes.

In this instance, His answer must have surprised them. "He called a child to Himself and set him before them, and said, 'Truly I say to you, unless you are converted and become like children, you will not enter the kingdom of heaven'" (18:2–3).

In order to humble them from the pride their question revealed, the Lord picked up a child and told them, "Unless you are converted and become like children"—that is, unless you turn from your foolish pride—"you will not enter the kingdom of heaven." No one enters the kingdom of heaven because he or she earned it or because he or she is worthy of it. The disciples' thinking about their place in the kingdom was entirely wrongheaded and backward. Christ continued in verse 4, "Whoever then humbles himself as this child"—with nothing to offer and no accomplishments or credentials to point to—"he is the greatest in the kingdom of heaven."

Having bashed their pride (at least temporarily), He followed with a shocking statement in verse 5. "And whoever receives one such child in

My name receives Me." He wasn't talking about showing hospitality to physical children. Rather, He used the child He was holding to illustrate childlike humility.

Believers are in God's kingdom because we humbled ourselves. We recognize the worthlessness of our own works and cling to the completed work of Christ. We are "the poor in spirit" (Matt. 5:3), who mourn over the great cost of our sin (5:4) and who "hunger and thirst for righteousness" that only Christ can provide (5:6). And having humbled ourselves, we are now the children of God. And we need to be reminded that when we come into one another's presence, we're having an encounter not merely with another redeemed soul but with Christ Himself.

How we treat other believers is how we treat Christ. Consider the members of your local church. How do you interact with them? Do you try to keep your distance from anyone in particular? Because the love you show to fellow believers—or the lack thereof—is what you're showing to Christ Himself. Someday, we will stand before God to give an account for how we treated fellow believers.

And if that doesn't give you pause, this will. In Matthew 18:6 Christ says, "But whoever causes one of these little ones who believe in Me to stumble, it would be better for him to have a heavy millstone hung around his neck, and to be drowned in the depth of the sea."

How you treat other believers is deadly serious. When you mistreat another believer, or cause them to stumble into sin, you're doing that to one in whom Christ dwells. And you would be better off dead than to cause another one in Christ to sin.

There is no room for disdain or ridicule within God's family. That might mean you have to show an extra measure of patience with some in the midst of their sanctification, or go out of your way to encourage and aid them in their pursuit of Christlikeness. And it means you can't hold a grudge against another believer—that you always have to forgive and work to repair the relationship. If you love Christ, then you must also love those He loves. Loving Christ necessarily entails loving His bride.

You have no excuse to look down on another believer. You have no excuse to treat others as less important or valuable than yourself. We all stood equally guilty before the cross. All of us were bought at the same price. And we were all granted the same righteousness that none of us earned. We cannot jockey for position in the kingdom of God. We are all equally precious, and eternally united, to Him.

Study Questions:

1. Why does the Bible speak of Christians as aliens, strangers, and citizens of another world? In practical terms, what does it mean to be heaven's colony?
2. What does it mean to "have the mind of Christ" (1 Cor. 2:16)? What impact should that have on your day-to-day life?
3. What does Paul mean when he says in Second Corinthians 5:21 that Jesus "became sin"?
4. Explain in your own words the doctrine of imputation.
5. If you're interacting with Christ when you interact with other believers, how should that affect your view of service to the church?

4

The Church and Purification

CONTINUING IN Matthew 18, we come to another foundational pillar of the redeemed church: purification. The Lord demands a pure church. Having been elected by Him for salvation, having been bought through the sacrifice of His Son, having been cloaked in His righteousness, and having been brought into eternal union with Him, we need to live in such a way that reflects His righteousness to the world around us.

Peter put it this way in his first epistle: "As obedient children, do not be conformed to the former lusts *which were yours* in your ignorance, but like the Holy One who called you, be holy yourselves also in all *your* behavior" (1 Pet. 1:14–15).

Put simply, we need to be holy because He is holy (1 Pet. 1:16).

Personal Purity

In Matthew 18, Christ illustrated the great lengths to which He wants His people to go to protect their purity.

> If your hand or your foot causes you to stumble, cut it off and throw it from you; it is better for you to enter life crippled or lame, than to have two hands or two feet and be cast into the eternal fire. If your eye causes you to stumble, pluck it out and throw it from you. It is better for you to enter life with one eye, than to have two eyes and be cast into the fiery hell. (18:8–9)

Jesus wasn't prescribing self-mutilation. Hacking off a foot or a hand does not get at the source of sin, which is the heart (James 1:14–15). Rather, He was using graphic hyperbole to declare the seriousness of our sin and the severity we must use to deal with it when it starts in our hearts.

And to be clear, He was saying that you must take drastic, radical steps to remove temptation from your life. In practical terms, cutting off your hand or your foot correlates to altering your life so that temptation is out of arm's reach. It might mean taking a longer route for your commute to avoid certain places, removing certain items from your home, or otherwise distancing yourself from a source of temptation—the command here is to find a way to cut off your access to it altogether.

In the same sense, plucking out an eye could mean cutting off your cable or your Internet access. It might be as simple as turning around your computer screen so everyone else in the room can see it—whatever steps you need to take to guard your eyes from anything that will lead you into temptation.

The Lord demands that His people take sin seriously. There is no tolerable amount of temptation that we can afford to face, no acceptable dalliances with sin and corruption. The world is overrun with opportunities for sin, and devising new delivery systems for temptation all the time.

As Jesus said, "Woe to the world because of its stumbling blocks! For it is inevitable that stumbling blocks come; but woe to that man through whom the stumbling block comes!" (Matt. 18:7). If you're inviting temptation into your own life, whether on purpose or just through carelessness, that "woe"—a pronouncement of grave judgment—applies to you.

We must guard our hearts in the fight against sin. And by God's grace, we're not in the fight alone.

Corporate Purity

Christ also instituted a system by which the people of His kingdom can hold each other accountable in our collective pursuit of holiness. In that sense, this is the first corporate instruction the Lord gives to His church. In Matthew 18:15, Jesus said, "If your brother sins, go and show him his fault in private; if he listens to you, you have won your brother."

It's worth noting that from the outset, the goal of church discipline is repentance and restoration. The point is not to vent your complaints about another believer or to somehow become a sanctified busybody. You bring your brother's or your sister's sin to that person's attention for the sake of helping him or her cut it out of his or her life. You do it as a service of love to other believers, for the sake of their spiritual growth and the testimony they present to the world. The only goal is their purity.

However, believers engaged in sin—and especially those living in open, unrepentant sin—may not respond in repentance to such loving confrontation. For that reason, the Lord continued, "But if he does not listen to you, take one or two more with you, so that BY THE MOUTH OF TWO OR THREE WITNESSES EVERY FACT MAY BE CONFIRMED" (18:16).

Because the goal is the other person's purity, you can't simply drop the issue if the initial effort was rebuffed. Taking another witness or two ratchets up the seriousness of the matter and will hopefully grab the sinning brother's or sister's attention in a way that the first discussion did not.

It also serves as a guard against petty, interpersonal arguments. Bringing witnesses means the matter can't be dismissed as an issue of "he said, she said." Nor will the facts of the matter be up for debate.

This was always the standard for God's people, going all the way back to the Mosaic law—in fact, Christ was partially quoting from Deuteronomy 19:15, "A single witness shall not rise up against a man on account of any iniquity or any sin which he has committed; on the evidence of two or three witnesses a matter shall be confirmed."

Again, the goal is not to build a case against the sinning brother or sister. It's to call that person to repent and return to a right relationship with the Lord. But, Jesus said, "If he refuses to listen to them, tell it to the church; and if he refuses to listen even to the church, let him be to you as a Gentile and a tax collector" (18:17).

If the professing believer persists in sin, you bring the matter before the whole church, urging them to likewise call that person to repentance. The full weight of the local body should be brought down on the believer's shoulders, for the sake of his or her soul.

God prizes the purity of His people and will not tolerate sin, so neither can His church. And if that effort fails, the person is to be put out of the church altogether, and urged to repent and believe—that's what it means to treat him or her "as a Gentile and a tax collector." You preach the gospel to the person the way you would to any unbeliever, because that's how the person is behaving. The person's unrepentant sin has made him or her like an outsider to God's family, and a threat to its purity. For the sake of his or her own soul, as well as for the sake of the rest of the church, the person must be put out of the fellowship.

Sometimes, when this final step has been completed, the sinner truly understands the weight of his or her sin. When the person is face-to-face with the consequences of his or her sinful actions and has been removed from the fellowship of the saints, he or she may finally appreciate the true need to repent. And by God's grace, some do.

At our church, we have enjoyed the rare privilege of welcoming back into fellowship some of those who previously had to be put out. It is a powerful testimony to the value of such ministry, as hard as it is, to see God's plan for church discipline accomplish its goal and bring about the repentance and restoration of a sinning brother or sister.

When I first came to Grace Community Church, I told an older pastor that I had never seen a church actually practice the process outlined in Matthew 18. And yet Scripture was so explicit, I couldn't imagine overlooking or sidestepping such clear instructions. I was convinced that we had to do what Christ commanded. But in a long speech, my friend warned me that I would destroy the church if I tried to follow the biblical teaching on church discipline—that people wouldn't tolerate it.

I simply responded that people who want themselves and their church to love Christ would see its value. People who want to be like Christ *welcome* all the help and encouragement they can find in the pursuit of Christlikeness—even when it comes in the form of a public confrontation. Christ wants a pure church, and the people who truly love Him likewise want to keep His church pure.

And just so God's people don't become overly obsessed with confronting one another, the Lord includes another command on the matter. In verse 21, Peter interjected a question. "Lord, how often shall my brother sin against me and I forgive him? Up to seven times?"

The rabbis had taught that you were to forgive someone up to three times. No doubt Peter thought he sounded magnanimous by doubling it and adding one.

Christ's response surely shocked him. "I do not say to you, up to seven times, but up to seventy times seven" (18:22). He made it clear that Peter's magnanimous estimate was pitifully low. And to be clear, Jesus was not limiting a believer's forgiveness to 490 occurrences. He was telling His disciples that their forgiveness should be limitless—that they should always be willing to forgive one another. As our Lord said to His disciples, "For if you forgive others for their transgressions, your heavenly Father will also forgive you. But if you do not forgive others, then your Father will not forgive your transgressions" (Matt. 6:14–15).

In the span of just a few verses, the Lord demanded that sin be confronted, but that the confrontation is to be balanced with a forgiving spirit among His people. And it makes sense that we would never withhold forgiveness from a brother or a sister in Christ if the point of confronting the sin were always repentance and restoration. If your goal is the other person's purity, you'll never struggle to forgive.

Swift Justice

On occasion, however, the Lord Himself will act swiftly to deal with sin in the midst of His people—which includes removing the sinner altogether. John referred to this as "a sin *leading* to death" (1 John 5:16).

Writing to the Corinthians, Paul explained that their abuse of the Lord's Supper had led to severe consequences. "For this reason many among you are weak and sick, and a number sleep" (1 Cor. 11:30), which is to say, they had died.

Earlier in the same epistle, regarding another sinning member of the church, Paul said, "*I have decided* to deliver such a one to Satan for the destruction of his flesh, so that his spirit may be saved in the day of the Lord Jesus" (5:5). God desires a pure church, and will act righteously to protect its purity.

Another vivid example of this is recorded in Acts 5. In the earliest days of the church, God showed His people how much He prized their purity. Acts 4 concludes with a testimony to the unity and fellowship of the early church.

> The congregation of those who believed were of one heart and soul; and not one of them claimed that anything belonging to him was his own, but all things were common property to them. . . . For there was not a needy person among them, for all who were owners of land or houses would sell them and bring the proceeds of the sales and lay them at the apostles' feet, and they would be distributed to each as any had need. (4:32, 34–35)

Luke even concluded the chapter by mentioning a specific man named Joseph (Barnabas) who sold a tract of land for the purpose of sharing the money with the rest of the church (4:36–37). While we find no record of pressure from the apostles to make such sacrifices, this generosity reflected the love in that first church.

But not everyone in the early church had such pure motives. Luke began chapter 5 with the cautionary tale of one couple. "But a man named Ananias, with his wife Sapphira, sold a piece of property, and kept back some of the price for himself, with his wife's full knowledge, and bringing a portion of it, he laid it at the apostles' feet" (Acts 5:1–2).

Clearly, these two wanted the public recognition for an act of self-sacrifice without actually making the full sacrifice they claimed. God revealed their wicked intentions in a public judgment.

> But Peter said, "Ananias, why has Satan filled your heart to lie to the Holy Spirit and to keep back some of the price of the land? While it remained *unsold*, did it not remain your own? And after it was sold, was it not under your control?

> Why is it that you have conceived this deed in your heart? You have not lied to men but to God." And as he heard these words, Ananias fell down and breathed his last; and great fear came over all who heard of it. The young men got up and covered him up, and after carrying him out, they buried him. (5:3–6)

In human terms, Ananias had committed what some might think of as a minor sin. He hadn't murdered anyone. He hadn't fallen into adultery, homosexuality, or some other kind of sexual immorality. He hadn't injured or robbed anyone. All he did was make a public claim about something he hadn't really done—he lied about the generosity of his gift.

But in that early church, God sent His people a lesson never to be forgotten, and killed Ananias right in the middle of the service. God wants a pure church. And in this case, He was the one to purify it. And His work was not yet finished.

> Now there elapsed an interval of about three hours, and his wife came in, not knowing what had happened. And Peter responded to her, "Tell me whether you sold the land for such and such a price?" And she said, "Yes, that was the price." Then Peter said to her, "Why is it that you have agreed together to put the Spirit of the Lord to the test? Behold, the feet of those who have buried your husband are at the door, and they will carry you out as well." And immediately she fell at his feet and breathed her last, and the young men came in and found her dead, and they carried her out and buried her beside her husband. And great fear came over the whole church, and over all who heard of these things. (5:7–11)

Just like her husband, Sapphira told a simple lie. And just like her husband, God struck her dead immediately. This was a powerful lesson for the rest of that church—God takes all sin seriously, and they needed to as well. He wants a pure church, and when He decides to, He will be the one to purify it.

The Lord's Work in His Church

God's purifying work in His church has continued to this day—and rarely does it involve striking people dead. Whenever a pastor or church leader has disqualified himself and been removed from ministry, or a believer's life has been upended by the consequences of his sin, God is at work disciplining His church.

John provided us with a stunning vision of this in the first chapter of Revelation. The apostle's vision of the glorified Christ standing in the middle of the lampstands depicts His ongoing work in the midst of His church. Key aspects of John's vision are directly related to the Lord's work of purifying His church.

John wrote, "His head and His hair were white like white wool, like snow; and His eyes were like a flame of fire. His feet were like burnished bronze, when it has been made to glow in a furnace" (Rev. 1:14–15).

The vision of Christ's head and hair "like white wool, like snow" is a picture of His purity and holiness. The Lord is completely without blemish. He doesn't merely meet the standard for holiness—He *is* the standard. He defines what it means to be holy, and He is the model that His people are supposed to pursue.

John also mentioned that Christ's "eyes were like a flame of fire." This is a picture of the Lord's penetrating gaze into His church. Nothing can be hidden from His sight. As the author of Hebrews put it, "There is no creature hidden from His sight, but all things are open and laid bare to the eyes of Him with whom we have to do" (Heb. 4:13). He sees through every façade, into the very heart of His church. And He knows your heart more thoroughly and accurately than you do. No sin goes unseen by Him, and no impurity escapes His notice.

John identifies Christ's feet that glowed "like burnished bronze," the feet of the sovereign Lord, as He executes judgment on those under His authority. But they aren't feet of flesh—they're made of blazing, molten metal. And with them the Lord is stamping out the impurities He finds in His church.

Obviously this is not final judgment, but the loving discipline that a father shows to his children. The author of Hebrews describes it this way:

> You have forgotten the exhortation which is addressed to you as sons, "My son, do not regard lightly the discipline of the Lord, nor faint when you are reproved by Him; for those whom the Lord loves He disciplines, and He scourges every son whom He receives." It is for discipline that you endure; God deals with you as with sons; for what son is there whom *his* father does not discipline? But if you are without discipline, of which all have become partakers, then you are illegitimate children and not sons. Furthermore, we had earthly fathers to discipline us, and we respected them; shall we not much rather be subject to the Father of spirits, and live? For they disciplined us for a short time as seemed best to them, but He *disciplines us for our* good, so that we may share His holiness. (Heb. 12:5–10)

The Lord desires pure churches. He calls churches to repent if they are not pure, as the letters to the seven churches in Revelation illustrate.

He warned the church at Pergamum, "Therefore repent; or else I am coming to you quickly, and I will make war against them with the sword of My mouth" (Rev. 2:16).

The church at Thyatira was following a false teacher—a self-proclaimed prophetess who was leading the believers into immorality. Regarding His judgment for her and those under her influence, the Lord said,

> I gave her time to repent, and she does not want to repent of her immorality. Behold, I will throw her on a bed *of sickness*, and those who commit adultery with her into great tribulation, unless they repent of her deeds. And I will kill her children with pestilence, and all the churches will know that I am He who searches the minds and hearts; and I will give to each one of you according to your deeds. (2:21–23)

In chapter 3, He confronted the church at Sardis. "So remember what you have received and heard; and keep it, and repent. Therefore if you do not wake up, I will come like a thief, and you will not know at what hour I will come to you" (3:3).

And the warning He gave to the church at Laodicea is a frightening reminder for every church: "Those whom I love, I reprove and discipline; therefore be zealous and repent" (3:19). Sanctification—both corporately and individually—is His will for the life of every church.

The Pastor's Burden for His People

The spiritual work of purifying the church is exclusively the Lord's. It's only through His power that any of us are saved in the first place. And only through the Holy Spirit working through His Word are we able to grow in Christlikeness. But the Lord does that work through shepherds—pastors and elders—to oversee, care for, lead, and discipline His sheep.

Paul provides us with an example of that pastoral duty in Second Corinthians. Writing to the church, which he loved but which gave him so much trouble, he said, "I am jealous for you with a godly jealousy; for I betrothed you to one husband, so that to Christ I might present you as a pure virgin" (2 Cor. 11:2).

Later, he expressed his trepidation about returning to them and finding them in sin.

> For I am afraid that perhaps when I come I may find you to be not what I wish and may be found by you to be not what you wish; that perhaps *there will be* strife, jealousy, angry tempers, disputes, slanders, gossip, arrogance, disturbances; I am afraid that when I come again my God may humiliate

> me before you, and I may mourn over many of those who have sinned in the past and not repented of the impurity, immorality and sensuality which they have practiced. (2 Cor. 12:20–21)

He warned them that he would take the sin he found among them seriously. "I have previously said when present the second time, and though now absent I say in advance to those who have sinned in the past and to all the rest *as well*, that if I come again I will not spare anyone" (2 Cor. 13:2).

Those are the words of a loving pastor. His heart was burdened for his sheep, but his love for them would not cloud his judgment. He was coming to deal with the sin in their midst. He was going to do his part to keep them pure.

Purity and Assurance

Paul urged them to get busy even before his return. He told them, "Test yourselves to see if you are in the faith; examine yourselves!" (12:5).

Thinking about that, I couldn't help but be drawn to a book written by a Puritan named Thomas Brooks, called *Heaven on Earth*. He wrote to believers, helping them understand how they could experience heaven on earth in a personal sense. We've considered that concept in terms of its collective application in the church. Brooks was focused on the individual application. Here's how he described it:

> To be in a state of true grace is to be miserable no more; it is to be happy for ever. A soul in this state is a soul near and dear to God. It is a soul much beloved, and very highly valued of God. It is a soul housed in God. It is a soul safe in everlasting arms. It is a soul fully and eminently interested in all the highest and noblest privileges. The being in a state of grace makes a man's condition happy, safe, and sure; but the seeing, the knowing of himself to be in such a state, is that which renders his life sweet and comfortable.[1]

You will not find heaven on earth if you don't know you're in a state of grace. Thomas Brooks was writing about assurance. The church is heaven on earth, and all who are true believers constitute the colony of heaven on earth. But those who have assurance are the ones who, as Brooks said, live in two heavens: the heaven above and the heaven within; that is, the heaven of being blessed by your own conscience.

> Now assurance is a reflex act of a gracious soul, whereby he clearly and evidently sees himself in a gracious, blessed, and happy state; it is a sensible feeling, and an experimental discerning of a man's being in a state of grace,

1 Thomas Brooks, *Heaven on Earth* (Edinburgh: Banner of Truth Trust, 2022), 7.

> and of his having a right to a crown of glory; and this rises from the seeing in himself the special, peculiar, and distinguishing graces of Christ, in the light of the Spirit of Christ, or from the testimony and report of the Spirit of God, "the Spirit bearing witness with his spirit, that he is a son, and an heir-apparent to glory," Rom. 8:16, 17.[2]

Sadly, many Christians do not enjoy the internal heaven. Brooks wrote,

> Assurance is the beauty and top of a Christian's glory in this life. It is usually attended with the strongest joy, with the sweetest comforts, and with the greatest peace. It is a pearl that most want, a crown that few wear. . . . A man may be a true believer, and yet would give all the world, were it in his power, to know that he is a believer. To have grace, and to be sure that we have grace, is glory upon the throne, it is heaven on this side of heaven.[3]

If you are in a state of grace but you have no assurance of that, that's a kind of hell. Individually, personally, we want heaven, heaven on earth, and heaven in our hearts.

Study Questions:

1. Why is the purity of the church important?
2. What lengths did God go to in order to keep His church pure in Acts 5?
3. What is the purpose of church discipline? Why do so many churches fail to practice it?
4. What is the relationship between purity and assurance?
5. Explain in your own words how you can be a purifying influence in your local church.

---

2 Brooks, 7.

3 Brooks, 8.

5

The Church and Revelation

God's word does not change. Psalm 119:89 extolls the immutable nature of Scripture by saying, "Forever, O Lord, Your word is settled in heaven." For all generations in all of human history, the Word of God is settled—it is permanent, fixed, and established in heaven. The point echoes again in verse 160, "The sum of Your word is truth, and every one of Your righteous ordinances is everlasting."

The prophet Isaiah put it this way, "The grass withers, the flower fades, but the word of our God stands forever" (Isa. 40:8). Peter quotes Isaiah to make the same point in his first epistle, "All flesh is like grass, and all its glory like the flower of grass. The grass withers, and the flower falls off, but the word of the Lord endures forever" (1 Pet. 1:24–25).

Even Jesus spoke of the everlasting quality of God's Word. "For truly I say to you, until heaven and earth pass away, not the smallest letter or stroke shall pass from the Law until all is accomplished" (Matt. 5:18). And again, "Heaven and earth will pass away, but My words will not pass away" (Matt. 24:35).

The Word of God is eternal, never altered and never changed. Nothing can be added to it, and nothing can be removed. In fact, that was the final warning in the Bible, at the end of Revelation. John pronounced a curse on anyone who would dare to edit God's Word in any way (Rev. 22:18–19). His truth is settled in heaven forever.

So, as we consider how the redeemed church operates as heaven on earth, we understand that our role is to simply bring the truth of God, settled in heaven, down to earth and live according to it.

In terms of the doctrinal truths that shape the church, nothing is more foundational than the Bible—God's revelation.

Be Conformed to the Word

One reality guarantees that the church will be heaven on earth, and it's that it is conformed to Scripture. That effectively becomes the theme of the instruction in two critical New Testament epistles, First and Second Timothy.

We've already looked at First Timothy 3:15, where Paul referred to the church as "the church of the living God, the pillar and support of the truth."

What truth? The truth settled forever in heaven as revealed on the pages of Scripture. Paul immediately followed that up in First Timothy 4 with this warning: "The Spirit explicitly says that in later times some will fall away from the faith, paying attention to deceitful spirits and doctrines of demons, by means of the hypocrisy of liars seared in their own conscience as with a branding iron" (4:1–2).

The implication is that these false teachers will go against the Scriptures. They might add to it or they might take away from it, or twist and misuse it, but the implication is clear that these people will not be faithful to the Word of God.

By holding fast to the truth and warning those under his care about the threat these false teachers represent, Paul said that Timothy "will be a good servant of Christ Jesus, *constantly* nourished on the words of the faith and of the sound doctrine which you have been following" (4:6).

The Word plays a crucial role in feeding and protecting the flock of God. By contrast, Paul wrote, "Have nothing to do with worldly fables" (4:7). Stay committed to the Scriptures, and avoid the myths of the world. In verse 11, Paul exhorted his apprentice, "Prescribe and teach these things"—that is, the truths revealed by God in His Word, and handed down to Timothy from the faithful teachers who taught him. The church will be like heaven when it submits to, conforms to, is faithful to, and proclaims the eternal Word of God.

Paul continued his words to Timothy in 4:13, "Until I come, give attention to the *public* reading of *Scripture*, to exhortation and teaching." And in verse 16, "Pay close attention to yourself and to your teaching; persevere in these things, for as you do this you will ensure salvation both for yourself and for those who hear you."

If a pastor wants his church to be everything God wants it to be, then he must live a godly life and faithfully teach His Word.

In First Timothy 6, Paul concluded his mentoring, "O Timothy, guard what has been entrusted to you, avoiding worldly *and* empty chatter *and* the opposing arguments of what is falsely called 'knowledge'—which some have professed and thus gone astray from the faith" (6:20–21). Fix your heart and mind on the truth, and remember the bad outcome that will occur if you become consumed with what passes for knowledge with the world.

Paul picked up this theme again early in his second epistle to Timothy. "Retain the standard of sound words which you have heard from me, in the faith and love which are in Christ Jesus. Guard, through the Holy Spirit who dwells in us, the treasure which has been entrusted to you" (1:13–14). I gave you the truth—hold fast to it. And faithfully instruct others in it, as well. "Remind *them* of these things, and solemnly charge *them* in the presence of God not to wrangle about words, which is useless *and leads* to the ruin of the hearers" (2:14).

This is no time for fancy oratory and clever speech. Paul prescribed just one objective: Preach the truth. "Be diligent to present yourself approved to God as a workman who does not need to be ashamed, accurately handling the word of truth. But avoid worldly *and* empty chatter, for it will lead to further ungodliness, and their talk will spread like gangrene" (2:15–17).

The church has one book, one revelation: the Bible. We do not adhere to the Bible and the Book of Mormon or the Bible and a copy of *Science and Health with a Key to the Scriptures*. We don't follow the Bible and the Catholic Apocrypha, or any other memoir or manifesto that the cults hold up as divinely inspired truth. We have one book—one authoritative Word of God. And it is sufficient for everything we need.

The All-Sufficient Scripture

In Psalm 19:7–9, David poetically extolled the sufficiency of Scripture. It's just three simple verses, but it imparts rich truths to us about the nature of God's Word. Of course, this is ultimately the Lord communicating to us through David's pen. And with an economy of words, He testifies to the everlasting qualities of His revealed truth.

> The law of the Lord is perfect, restoring the soul;
> The testimony of the Lord is sure, making wise the simple.
> The precepts of the Lord are right, rejoicing the heart;
> The commandment of the Lord is pure, enlightening the eyes.
> The fear of the Lord is clean, enduring forever;
> The judgments of the Lord are true; they are righteous altogether.

With the continual refrain "of the Lord," we can have no doubt who the author of Scripture is. God revealed Himself to us. The human mind cannot reach out of the confines of time and space and ascend to the eternal mind of God. God must break in with His own self-disclosure, and He has done that in the pages of His Word.

And David wanted us to see it for all that it is. Like a precious gem, he wanted us to carefully examine it in all its glorious facets. It is law, testimony, precepts, commandment, fear, and judgments. You can look at Scripture in all those ways.

Six characteristics are also indicated: God's Word is perfect, sure, right, pure, clean, and true. And then he showed us six effects. It revives the soul, makes wise the simple, rejoices the heart, enlightens the eyes, endures forever, and produces comprehensive righteousness. These are sweeping, powerful statements about the sufficiency of Scripture. We'll dig into them one at a time.

The first perspective on Scripture is as a law (19:7). That is to say, it's God's laws for man's life. God, as the Designer, has written the manufacturer's manual, explaining how human beings are to operate at maximum level of blessing. His Word tells us what it takes to live a life to the full. It educates and prepares us, telling us how to live now and forever.

Scripture is the manual that presents God's laws for human life. And David tells us it is "perfect." That's not perfect in the sense of contrasting with imperfection. Rather, it's perfect in the sense of being complete. God's law is perfect in that nothing was left out or excluded. Jude refers to it as "the faith which was once for all handed down to the saints" (Jude 3). Everything God wants you to know is here. It's comprehensive. It thoroughly covers everything necessary for life and godliness (2 Pet. 1:3).

And the effect of this complete revelation for human life is that it "[restores] the soul" (Ps. 19:7). The word for "soul" refers to the inner person—the real you. David was saying that the Word of God is comprehensive, and it is directed toward restoring or reviving the inner person.

That means Scripture is totally transforming. It gives life to the dead. And given that all people are born dead in their trespasses and sins (Eph. 2:1), the only hope for life is through the Word of God. James wrote that God "brought us forth by the word of truth" (James 1:18). He makes us new creations through the power of His Word.

Scripture alone has the power to regenerate the spiritually dead human soul and give it eternal life. We are begotten by the Word of Truth. We are given life through the glorious revelation of the gospel in the Bible.

Next, David wanted us to consider God's Word as "the testimony of the Lord" (Ps. 19:7). This refers to God's own self-disclosure to us. He gives testimony to who He is and what He has done. It's what He has revealed to us about Himself. And it is "sure," or trustworthy.

In a world of lies and deception, where people are fortified in destructive and damning error, only one source of truth can deliver them. In Second Corinthians 10:4, Paul wrote, "The weapons of our warfare are not of the flesh, but divinely powerful for the destruction of fortresses."

Paul was describing the nature of true spiritual warfare. Christians don't directly engage in battling the demons; we make war with their satanic ideologies. The fortresses he described are "speculations and every lofty thing raised up against the knowledge of God" (10:5). We are battling those anti-God ideologies that run contrary to Scripture.

The word Paul used to describe these fortresses could also refer to a prison or a tomb. And that's the progression that people caught in these systems will endure—they think they're in a protected ideological stronghold that is really a spiritual prison, and it will one day be their tomb unless they are revived and set free by the truth of Scripture concerning the Lord Jesus Christ.

In that sense, we are spiritual liberators. That's what evangelism is, and it's a mental battle, not an emotional one. How do you attack the errors in which people are imprisoned? The only way to attack error is with the truth. We bring the power of God's Word to bear because it is sure, trustworthy truth.

I love how David described the effect of God's trustworthy testimony, "making wise the simple" (Ps. 19:7). The Hebrew word for "simple" refers to an open door. It describes someone who can't keep anything out or anything in. People today brag about having an open mind, but often that only means that they have no discernment. God's Word takes people in that open and defenseless state and makes them wise—makes them skilled at living.

Verse 8 provides us with two more facets of God's revelation. "The precepts of the Lord" is another way to say *principles*. David had doctrine in mind here. And he said these biblical precepts are "right"—not in the sense of right versus wrong, although they are, but right in the sense of the course they provide us to follow. The doctrines God presents to us in His Word put us on the divine path of life.

Psalm 119:105 says, "Your word is a lamp to my feet and a light to my path." God's Word is the light and the lamp, but it also sets the path. The doctrine revealed in Scripture sets the path for our lives. And the effect of following the path of God's doctrine is that it rejoices the heart (Ps. 19:8).

If you want to find real joy, walk in a righteous path. Jesus said, "Blessed are those who hear the word of God and observe it" (Luke 11:28). He said, "These things I have spoken to you so that My joy may be in you, and that your joy may be made full" (John 15:11). First John 1:4 says, "These things we write, so that our joy may be made complete."

God has given everyone a mechanism called a conscience (Rom. 2:15). Its purpose is to affirm or condemn. And we all know the experience of a guilty conscience. But when you walk in the righteous path established by God's Word, your conscience excuses you rather than accuses you. You experience the joy of an obedient life. The Word of God provides that for you—it shows you the path to walk.

Throughout his ministry, the apostle Paul was maligned, slandered, and accused of all kinds of wickedness. The false teachers in Corinth were particularly brutal. They assaulted his character to raise doubts in the minds of the Corinthian believers. They claimed he had a hidden life of secret sin; that he was in the ministry for money or to take advantage of women. They mocked his teaching and his personality. They went after everything they could to diminish his influence in Corinth. Here's how he responded to their lying abuse: "Our proud confidence is this: the testimony of our conscience, that in holiness and godly sincerity, not in fleshly wisdom but in the grace of God, we have conducted ourselves in the world, and especially toward you" (2 Cor. 1:12).

That's how you want to live. No matter the arrows and darts that come at you, a clear conscience cannot be thwarted. No attack, no matter how vicious, can steal your joy if you are faithfully following the Lord's precepts. If that's how you want to live, walk the righteous path established by God's Word.

In Psalm 19:8, David also referred to Scripture as "the commandment of the Lord." This is the view of the Bible as mandates, absolute commands. It's a look at the authority of Scripture.

Our contemporary culture doesn't have a high view of authority and instructions. Too many operate as an authority unto themselves. But the commandments of God's Word are not mere suggestions—they are His unquestionable instructions for our lives.

David characterized these commandments as "pure" (19:8). But the emphasis wasn't on their spotless or sinless nature. Rather, it referred to their lucidity. He was saying that the Lord's commandments are clear—that they are understandable. Today, the church is seeing an attack on the clarity or perspicuity of God's Word. People will pay lip service to its authority but then undercut it by claiming it's too complex or outdated to make sense today.

That's nothing more than a ploy to excuse their unbelief and rebellion. Why would God give us revelation that we couldn't make sense of? What good is an inspired Word of God if it is inscrutable? It would be pointless. No, God is able to communicate to us clearly, and He has. His Word is crystal clear, and for anyone who will study it faithfully, its clarity will penetrate the heart and mind. Note the progression that David presented to us—the Word first transforms us, then it brings discernment and wisdom, and then comes joy and enlightenment.

Verse 9 presents us with the final two views of Scripture. The first is "the fear of the Lord." David was not talking about terror, but adoration. This is the "fear" of adoration, exaltation, praise, and worship. On top of everything else David showed us, the Bible is also a manual for worship. And he says it's "clean"—that is, it's unstained. It's flawless.

Everything human has a measure of corruption to it. But not God's Word. It's perfect, complete, and flawless. And that's why it will endure forever (19:9).

Along with the attack on the perspicuity of the Word today, there's a similar assault on its relevance. In this case, people will say they can understand what it means; they just don't believe it is applicable to life today. They think somehow society has outgrown God's Word; that the world is too sophisticated and too complex for a book from at least 2000 years ago.

But the truth of God's Word is transcendent. It's not bound to one time period or one culture. It is always relevant, to all people, at all times. I've had the privilege to travel all over the world and speak to people in almost every imaginable situation. And never once did I have to look outside the pages of Scripture for something to say to them. It is always true and always applicable. It doesn't need to be modified or manipulated—it just needs to be unleashed. It is always powerful, and it endures forever.

Finally, David points us to one more facet of God's Word. He calls it "the judgments of the Lord" (19:9). The Bible is the collection of divine adjudications from the Judge of the whole earth. It's handed down from the One who presides on the bench over all creation. The Word renders God's judgments—He has clearly laid them out.

David said the quality of these judgments is "true" (19:9). It's put simply but beautifully. The truth is what matters, in the end. I have no time for fictions, myths, fables, and tall tales. I'm not interested in lies and deceptions. I want the truth. And the Word of God is absolutely true.

Moreover, David said, "They are righteous altogether" (19:9). That simply means they produce comprehensive righteousness because they are true. God's judgments are entirely trustworthy. He will always tell you the way it really is. You don't have to second-guess the Lord's judgments. What He has said is always true, always right, and always reliable.

This is God's own testimony to the sufficiency of His Word. It is perfect, sure, right, pure, clean, and true. It totally transforms the inner person. It makes the undiscerning and naïve skilled in wisdom. It produces true, deep, lasting joy. It enlightens the eyes. It is eternally relevant, enduring forever. And it produces comprehensive righteousness.

That's why David said, "They are more desirable than gold, yes, than much fine gold; sweeter also than honey and the drippings of the honeycomb" (19:10).

God's Word is desirable and sweet. It is your greatest possession and your greatest pleasure. It's also your greatest protector ("By them your servant is warned") and your greatest provider ("In keeping them there is great reward," 19:11).

God's Word is also your greatest purifier. "Who can discern *his* errors? Acquit me of hidden faults. Also keep back Your servant from presumptuous *sins*; let them not rule over me; then I will be blameless, and I shall be acquitted of great transgression" (19:12–13). As the psalmist wrote, "Your word I have treasured in my heart, that I may not sin against You" (119:11).

David closed Psalm 19 with this: "Let the words of my mouth and the meditation of my heart be acceptable in Your sight, O Lord, my rock and my Redeemer" (19:14). This prayerful request is a reference to Joshua 1:7–9, where God commanded His people,

> Only be strong and very courageous; be careful to do according to all the law which Moses My servant commanded you; do not turn from it to the right or to the left, so that you may have success wherever you go. This book of the law shall not depart from your mouth, but you shall meditate on it day and night, so that you may be careful to do according to all that is written in it; for then you will make your way prosperous, and then you will have success. Have I not commanded you? Be strong and courageous! Do not tremble or be dismayed, for the Lord your God is with you wherever you go.

God's Word is sufficient for all our needs. Through it, He saves and sanctifies us and unleashes His truth and power in our lives.

Why We Preach the Word

In the Old Testament, God made a powerful promise through the prophet Isaiah.

> For as the rain and the snow come down from heaven, and do not return there without watering the earth and making it bear and sprout, and furnishing seed to the sower and bread to the eater; so will My word be which goes forth from My mouth; it will not return to Me empty, without accomplishing what I desire, and without succeeding *in the matter* for which I sent it. (Isa. 55:10–11)

This is an encouraging guarantee from the Lord. His Word will accomplish everything He intends it to do. It is the means through which He does His work. God has a plan, and He will work that plan through the proclamation of His Word. And it cannot fail.

With that in mind, we turn back to Second Timothy 3. Paul reminded his apprentice,

> From childhood you have known the sacred writings which are able to give you the wisdom that leads to salvation through faith which is in Christ Jesus. All Scripture is inspired by God and profitable for teaching, for reproof, for correction, for training in righteousness; so that the man of God may be adequate, equipped for every good work. (3:15–17)

The Bible is God's inspired Word—He breathed it out. And what does it do? How does it function according to His plan, for His intended purpose?

First of all, Paul identifies it as "the sacred writings which are able to give you the wisdom that leads to salvation through faith which is in Christ Jesus." How do we evangelize? How do we lead people to salvation? We use "the sacred writings," which bring sinners to the saving knowledge of the Lord.

The Word of God is the tool of salvation; it is the instrument through which He grows His kingdom. Christ made that clear in the gospel of John. "Truly, truly, I say to you, he who hears My word, and believes Him who sent Me, has eternal life, and does not come into judgment, but has passed out of death into life" (5:24). Not long after that, He reiterated, "It is the Spirit who gives life; the flesh profits nothing; the words that I have spoken to you are spirit and life" (6:63).

All the clever strategies for evangelism—all the surveys and studies to determine people's felt needs—they don't accomplish anything. Appealing to the flesh profits nothing. The Word alone does the work. Scripture alone gives spiritual life to the spiritually dead.

John closed his gospel with the affirmation, "These things have been written so that you may believe that Jesus is the Christ, the Son of God; and that believing you may have life in His name" (20:31). God wrote the Bible, He gave us His Word, so that you could have eternal life. As Romans 10:17 says, "Faith *comes* from hearing, and hearing by the word of Christ." Peter put it this way: "You have been born again not of seed which is perishable but imperishable, *that is*, through the living and enduring word of God" (1 Pet. 1:23).

Paul testified to the same power of the Word working in the Thessalonian believers. "For this reason we also constantly thank God that when you received the word of God which you heard from us, you accepted *it* not as the word of men, but *for* what it really is, the word of God, which also performs its work in you who believe" (1 Thess. 2:13). It not only saves—it continues to work powerfully in those who believe.

He highlighted that quality in Paul's exhortation to Timothy. Not only does God's Word produce salvation, it is "profitable for teaching" (2 Tim. 3:16)—it establishes doctrine. Paul's not talking about a process of teaching, but a body of content: the truth. Scripture is the body of revealed truth that Paul passed on to Timothy and instructed him to carefully guard and faithfully preach to those under his leadership.

The Bible is filled with eternal, unchanging, objective, propositional truth. It is inexcusable that so much time is wasted in churches today trying to exegete the culture, when God's Word is sitting right there, alive and powerful to transform lives. If you truly know what Scripture is able to accomplish, how could you give people anything else?

The knowledge of God's Word forms our entire theology; it informs our view of everything in the natural and the supernatural world. That's why the Bible instructs us over and over again to renew our minds with the Word (Rom. 12:2; Eph. 4:23). Knowing, understanding, and believing the truth has a continually transforming effect in our lives.

Christ told a group of Sadducees questioning Him about marriage in heaven, "You are mistaken, not understanding the Scriptures nor the power of God" (Matt. 22:29). The power of God is released through Scripture only when it is rightly divided and when you believe. The power of the Word unleashed in your life, when accurately understood, is the power that establishes a set of convictions by which you can live to your own blessing and to the glory of God.

Paul pointed out a third function of the Word in Second Timothy 3:16. Scripture is profitable not only for salvation and doctrine, but "for reproof." God's Word refutes. It rebukes. It convicts and convinces. This is the other side of teaching the truth—the Bible also exposes error.

When you preach the Word of God, you are bound to make some people uncomfortable. I am frequently asked if I worry about offending people. Of course not—if anything, I live to offend people with the truth, because that's the work of the Word. Scripture exposes their error. It confronts their deceptions. It unmasks every lie. That may be painful and offensive, but it is necessary.

The author of Hebrews provides us with an amazing testimony to the reproving, confronting power of Scripture. "The word of God is living and active and sharper than any two-edged sword, and piercing as far as the division of soul and spirit, of both joints and marrow, and able to judge the thoughts and intentions of the heart" (Heb. 4:12).

God's Word cuts right to the bone; it pierces your soul. It's dynamic and accurate, penetrating to the innermost recesses of the heart. It sifts. It analyzes. It reveals emotions, attitudes, thoughts, and behaviors. God does not miss anything or any one with His Word.

And sinners hate that. "Everyone who does evil hates the Light, and does not come to the Light for fear that his deeds will be exposed" (John 3:20). But that painful confrontation, that uncomfortable exposure is a necessary exercise. Because the rebuking, reproving work of the Word leads to its next function: correction (2 Tim. 3:16). This is the work of straightening you up, of thoroughly restoring you to a right position and perspective. God's Word will break you down, and it will put you back together in far better condition.

In John 15:3, Jesus talked about this function of His Word. He told His disciples, "You are already clean because of the word which I have spoken to you." Not only does Scripture expose your sin, it cleans you up. It corrects you.

Paul referred to this process in Ephesians 5:25–27. The apostle described the work of Christ to illustrate the sacrificial, protective love of a husband for his wife.

> Christ also loved the church and gave Himself up for her, so that He might sanctify her, having cleansed her by the washing of water with the word, that He might present to Himself the church in all her glory, having no spot

or wrinkle or any such thing; but that she would be holy and blameless.

The work of the Word isn't cruel—it's not out to destroy. It confronts error so that it can correct, build up, and ultimately sanctify.

In Second Timothy 3:16, Paul refers to the final function of Scripture as "training in righteousness." This is the full work of God's Word. It tears you down, rebuilds you, and trains you in the right direction. It is constantly steering you in the path of godliness. As Peter says, "Like newborn babies, long for the pure milk of the word, so that by it you may grow in respect to salvation" (1 Pet. 2:2).

Paul described the ultimate goal of this work. The Word assaults and offends you; it sets you on the correct course, and shows you how to walk in faithfulness "so that the man of God may be adequate, equipped for every good work" (2 Tim. 3:17). The ultimate goal is stimulating your spiritual growth and maximizing your usefulness for the work of the kingdom.

Flat, trivial, shallow preaching won't make you complete in Christ. No formula, no clever slogan, and no human wisdom will make you capable or competent in the work He has set aside for you. If you want to be spiritually prepared and proficient, you need to sit under the faithful proclamation of God's truth. Scripture alone is able to break you down and build you back up as a new creation. The Bible is God's only instrument for transforming His people.

All of that leads up to Paul's final command to Timothy.

> I solemnly charge you in the presence of God and of Christ Jesus, who is to judge the living and the dead, and by His appearing and His kingdom: *preach the word*; be ready in season *and* out of season; reprove, rebuke, exhort, with great patience and instruction. For the time will come when they will not endure sound doctrine; but *wanting* to have their ears tickled, they will accumulate for themselves teachers in accordance to their own desires, and will turn away their ears from the truth and will turn aside to myths. (2 Tim. 4:1–4)

The King of the kingdom is watching. Now is the time to faithfully execute the task for which He called you. Preach the Word.

We live in an age when churches are full of professing believers who cannot endure or tolerate sound doctrine. They want to have their ears tickled, and there are plenty of hirelings willing and eager to give them what they want. God's true church must stand apart from these charlatans and hucksters. We must hold fast to the Word.

The defining and distinguishing mark of God's church is the complete submission to the authority of His truth, forever settled in heaven, and unleashed through the faithful proclamation of His Word.

Study Questions:

1. Why is Scripture the ultimate authority for the church?
2. What other worldly influences compete to replace Scripture as the authority in the church? What threats do they pose?
3. Explain in your own words how Scripture is sufficient for life and godliness. Does your life reflect a commitment to its sufficiency?
4. Why must the Word of God be preached and taught? What are the results when it is not faithfully proclaimed?
5. Explain in your own words the danger of depending on human cleverness and ingenuity rather than Scripture alone for the work of evangelism.

6

The Church and Restoration

YEARS AGO, SHORTLY after the fall of the Soviet Union, I traveled to Kazakhstan to speak at a pastors' conference. About 1,700 pastors poured into the auditorium because events like this had never been allowed before. I was scheduled to teach all day for six straight days, unpacking the doctrines of the church.

Midway through this amazing week, the leaders called me into a room and said, "We have a question. When do you get to the good part?"

That was a little discouraging to hear, because I had already taught for something like twenty hours. So I said somewhat sheepishly, "Well, I don't know. What is the good part?"

They immediately responded, "It's what the Lord has planned for us in the future."

Those dear people lived a hardscrabble existence. They had persevered under Communist rule, but even though they were now free from that oppression, they still lived very difficult lives. I remember it rained all week, which was good news for them. They had massive cauldrons in the back of the church to catch the rain, and they threw whatever they could find into those giant pots, so we had rainwater soup with vegetables and potatoes all week. It was the kind of rough, trying lifestyle that would fix your mind on what Christ has prepared for you in eternity.

Without a doubt, that is the good part. And we spent one of the last days of that conference going over all God's promises for His people in the future. We rejoiced in the prewritten history of Christ's return, the glories of God's eternal kingdom, and all He has in store for us.

No matter where God's people live, or what circumstances we have to endure, we should always be looking forward to the return of Christ. Jesus is coming back. He will bring about the fulfillment and the culmination of all things, and He could arrive at any time. God's people are united in the hope of Christ's return, to deliver them into His eternal kingdom, to establish His rule over the world for a thousand years, and to ultimately reign in the new heaven and earth.

Concluding our list of doctrines that shape and uphold the redeemed church, we need to consider the restoration of all things and that begins with Christ's return.

SILENCE ON THE SECOND COMING

For many believers, apparently, understanding the Second Coming doesn't seem to be important. It has been misinterpreted through the years, leaving many in unnecessary confusion, while turning others off to the doctrine altogether. But the truth cannot be twisted or ignored. The Lord expects us to know what He has revealed—we are accountable for it. More than that, we need to understand His Second Coming because it glorifies Him, and it motivates us to live in the hopeful expectation of His return.

The Second Coming of Christ should be the best news for a believer. It sits at the heart of your worldview, coloring everything you look forward to in the future. God has already written the end of the story. We can read how this planet comes to its end, how the universe is destroyed and remade, and the future that awaits humanity. It's all in the pages of Scripture, and we can follow it detail by detail. The church's relative silence or lack of clarity on the topic makes no sense in light of Scripture's revelation of the specifics of eschatology.

There are countless theories about what's going to happen to the earth in the coming decades and centuries and what disasters may befall us in the near future and beyond. You can find the most frantic, bizarre, ridiculous, nonsensical, far-fetched notions of how the world will meet its demise. You could turn to those who debate how soon the planet will expire and what humans might do to hold off the cataclysm.

The most common theme throughout all the various hypotheses is fear. People fear that we're ruining the earth—that we have already destroyed it and that we're living on borrowed time. They live in fear that its resources are running out, that it is overcrowded, and that it's spinning out of control toward inevitable disaster.

God's people don't have to live with such fears. We don't have to worry about what will happen to the world—we can look to the pages of Scripture and read exactly what God has decreed and how it will happen. We can know for certain that it won't be destroyed by Satan, by men, or by any weapon, contaminant, or disaster that mankind could unleash. God's Word is clear: The world will be destroyed by Christ. It will be judged first and then destroyed by the Son of God.

Most of the panic over the planet's demise and the supposed threat that humans pose to their own existence are devised to control people through fear. That's why we keep outliving predictions about the next ice age, melting ice caps, climate change, and the exhaustion of natural resources and fossil fuels.

God's people can see through all of that hyperbolic nonsense if they simply avail themselves of the truth He has revealed in His Word. We can eagerly look forward to the "good part"—to the fulfillment of His plan of redemption. We can glorify Him by anticipating Christ's return and the restoration of all things.

And the Bible is neither vague nor equivocal regarding the Second Coming. More than two hundred prophecies in the Old Testament relate to Christ's return, and more than three hundred references relate to it in the New Testament. It's a staple of biblical revelation and doctrine. God has not been vague or mysterious about His plans. But in spite of that extensive revelation, much confusion and skepticism exist among God's people.

No doubt some of that has to do with the criticism of the world and the fear of other people. In his second epistle, Peter anticipated that very issue, and attempted to instill some confidence in his readers. "Know this first of all, that in the last days"—which include the days we're living in now—"mockers will come with *their* mocking, following after their own lusts, and saying, 'Where is the promise of His coming?'" (2 Pet. 3:3–4). The world is full of taunting voices that mockingly ask where the Son of God has gone, and why it has taken Him so long to return. They heap their scorn on believers for what they see as foolish, empty hope.

They say, "For ever since the fathers fell asleep, all continues just as it was from the beginning of creation" (3:4). This is the principle of uniformity—the idea that nature has never changed; that the world and everything in it operates by natural laws that have remained constant. Because they have never witnessed any kind of cataclysmic act of divine judgment in the past, they refuse to believe that one is coming in the future.

Peter explained that this assumption is folly. "For when they maintain this, it escapes their notice that by the word of God *the* heavens existed long ago and *the* earth was formed out of water and by water, through which the world at that time was destroyed, being flooded with water" (3:5–6).

He exposed the glaring flaw in their thinking—that they conveniently ignored the universal flood that destroyed the entire human race, except

Noah and his family. In spite of what they would like to believe, things have not always continued as they were from the beginning. The world was destroyed by water.

Peter was not finished. "But by His word the present heavens and earth are being reserved for fire, kept for the day of judgment and destruction of ungodly men" (2. Pet. 3:7). And if you're persuaded by doubts because it has been a couple thousand years of waiting, he added in verse 8, "But do not let this one *fact* escape your notice, beloved, that with the Lord one day is like a thousand years, and a thousand years like one day." God does not reckon time as we do, and it's foolish to think you know better than He does how long He should tarry.

Peter even explained that we should see the time Christ's return has taken as a great mercy. "The Lord is not slow about His promise, as some count slowness, but is patient toward you, not wishing for any to perish but for all to come to repentance" (3:9).

God isn't slow to return, He is gracious in that He continues to grant sinners time to repent. He's withholding His final judgment, the horrors of which Peter described. "But the day of the Lord will come like a thief, in which the heavens will pass away with a roar and the elements will be destroyed with intense heat, and the earth and its works will be burned up" (3:10).

In verse 12 he added, "The heavens will be destroyed by burning, and the elements will melt with intense heat!" Essentially, this is an atomic destruction. The whole planet and the whole universe are made of atoms, and they will explode in an unimaginable act of destruction by God's hand.

In Second Thessalonians 1, Paul points ahead to a day

> When the Lord Jesus will be revealed from heaven with His mighty angels in flaming fire, dealing out retribution to those who do not know God and to those who do not obey the gospel of our Lord Jesus. These will pay the penalty of eternal destruction, away from the presence of the Lord and from the glory of His power. (1:7–9)

People today are anxious about the future, but they are fearful for the wrong reasons. They worry about potential human-made or natural disasters that won't amount to anything, while blithely ignoring the terrifying truth that God's violent, destructive judgment is looming. Humans can do nothing to hasten or delay the world's end by even a second. The universe's lifespan is entirely up to God, and He has chosen exactly when He will unleash the fury of His judgment.

By the time the world realizes it's coming, it will be too late. Jesus described what that day will be like.

> There will be signs in sun and moon and stars, and on the earth dismay among nations, in perplexity at the roaring of the sea and the waves, men fainting from fear and the expectation of the things which are coming upon the world; for the powers of the heavens will be shaken. Then they will see the SON OF MAN COMING IN A CLOUD with power and great glory. (Luke 21:25–27)

The Lord's arrival will terrify humanity. In Revelation 6, John wrote that men will cry out "to the mountains and to the rocks, 'Fall on us and hide us from the presence of Him who sits on the throne, and from the wrath of the Lamb; for the great day of their wrath has come, and who is able to stand?'" (6:16–17).

"But," Jesus continued in Luke 21:28, "When these things begin to take place, straighten up and lift up your heads, because your redemption is drawing near." For the world, the Second Coming represents final judgment and destruction. But for believers, it is the final act of redemption.

In the upper room, Jesus encouraged His disciples.

> Do not let your heart be troubled; believe in God, believe also in Me. In My Father's house are many dwelling places; if it were not so, I would have told you; for I go to prepare a place for you. If I go and prepare a place for you, I will come again and receive you to Myself, that where I am, there you may be also. (John 14:1–3)

Christ is coming back, having prepared a place for His own in His presence in the glory of heaven. He is coming back to take His church home. This is the believer's great hope. It transcends whatever we may be called to endure in this fleeting life. Despite whatever struggles we might suffer through here, we will all be gathered together as the eternal bride of Christ, to live with Him forever in the Father's heavenly household.

The Rapture and Readiness

The Thessalonian church was a body of faithful believers. Paul commended them for their "work of faith," their "labor of love," and their "steadfastness of hope in our Lord Jesus Christ" (1 Thess. 1:3). The gospel had come to them "in power and in the Holy Spirit and with full conviction" (1:5), and they "received the word in much tribulation with the joy of the Holy Spirit" (1:6), such that they "became an example to all the believers in Macedonia and in Achaia" (1:7). "The word of the Lord . . . sounded forth" from them throughout the region (1:8). They had been truly and totally transformed by the Word, having "turned to God from idols to serve a living and true God" (1:9). And they nurtured the hope of the Second Coming, "[waiting] for His Son from heaven, whom He raised from the dead, that is Jesus, who rescues us from the wrath to come" (1:10).

That faithful, little church was waiting in the eager anticipation of Christ's return, just as we are today. We watch for Him to return to rescue us before holy, destructive wrath arrives.

In First Thessalonians 4, Paul informed and encouraged their hope—and ours—with this description of the day we eagerly await.

> For the Lord Himself will descend from heaven with a shout, with the voice of *the* archangel and with the trumpet of God, and the dead in Christ will rise first. Then we who are alive and remain will be caught up together with them in the clouds to meet the Lord in the air, and so we shall always be with the Lord. Therefore comfort one another with these words. (1 Thess. 4:16–18)

The Lord is coming to gather His people. Living believers will be caught up together with the resurrected saints who died in Christ, and the Lord will take His redeemed church to heaven. Paul wanted the Thessalonians to remind each other of this reality and to share in the comfort and hope it supplied. We are to do the same for one another today.

The day Paul describes in First Thessalonians 4 is called the rapture, from a Latin term that means, "to catch away." The Lord will return in the air to claim His own and take them to heaven. This will remove the restraint of the church from the world, and hell literally will break loose on earth. Satanic forces will overrun the world, with demons belching forth from the pit, and sin dominating the world. In fact, Satan will wield vicious, violent authority over the entire earth through the Antichrist.

This is the period known as the tribulation, when the world will suffer the unfolding judgments described in Revelation 6–18. That will culminate in the massive, global battle of Armageddon, as the forces of the world will gather against Christ, who will return from heaven with His glorified saints and the angels, to destroy the wicked and establish His kingdom on earth for a thousand years (Rev. 19, 20).

And at the end of those thousand years, Satan will be released to gather all unbelievers for one final rebellion, which will be stamped out by the Lord. Then He will destroy the entire universe to replace it with the new heavens and the new earth (Rev. 21, 22), where His righteous redeemed will live forever. That's what the Bible pre-records about the future judgment God will unleash, and His plan for the glorification of His people.

So the rapture of the church is the next event on God's redemptive calendar. Christ's return is the beginning of the end. We just don't know when He is coming. And we shouldn't—it's not for us to know. God has commanded His church to live in the active anticipation of His return. In His great Olivet discourse, Jesus pointed His disciples to many of the signs that would mark His return and described some of the judgments that would follow. But He also exhorted them to always be ready.

> Therefore be on the alert, for you do not know which day your Lord is coming. But be sure of this, that if the head of the house had known at what time of the night the thief was coming, he would have been on the alert and would not have allowed his house to be broken into. For this reason you also must be ready; for the Son of Man is coming at an hour when you do not think *He will.* (Matt. 24:42–44)

We don't look ahead to the end of the world with fear or terror, but with joyous anticipation. And along with that, we feel a renewed sense of urgency to seize the opportunities we have to advance the kingdom, as God mercifully holds back His wrath so that more may repent and believe.

Living in Light of the Lord's Return

So the calling of the church is to live in light of Christ's return. We are not here to solve the world's political and social problems. We are not meant to win a culture war or lay hold of the levers of political power. We're not trying to salvage or fix the world; that can't be done. This world is reserved for fire.

But we can make the most of the time we have been given, and live in the expectant hope of our Lord's return. Sadly, many Christians need to be reminded of that. They've grown complacent and self-centered. They live earthbound lives, caught up in the cares of this world. The New Testament writers recognized that danger and reminded their readers of the Lord's imminent return and how it should shape their lives. The church today would do well to heed their exhortations.

> See how great a love the Father has bestowed on us, that we would be called children of God; and *such* we are. For this reason the world does not know us, because it did not know Him. Beloved, now we are children of God, and it has not appeared as yet what we will be. We know that when He appears, we will be like Him, because we will see Him just as He is. (1 John 3:1–2)

Even the faithful Thessalonians were encouraged to remember that, "The day of the Lord will come just like a thief in the night" (1 Thess. 5:2). "So then," Paul wrote, "let us not sleep as others do, but let us be alert and sober" (5:6).

He reminded them that they didn't need to fear divine judgment. "For God has not destined us for wrath, but for obtaining salvation through our Lord Jesus Christ, who died for us, so that whether we are awake or asleep, we will live together with Him. Therefore encourage one another and build up one another, just as you also are doing" (5:9–11).

We need to wait for Christ just like the Thessalonians, encouraging and building each other up in our expectant hope of the glories to come.

Paul provided us with a similar reminder in Titus 2.

> For the grace of God has appeared, bringing salvation to all men, instructing us to deny ungodliness and worldly desires and to live sensibly, righteously and godly in the present age, looking for the blessed hope and the appearing of the glory of our great God and Savior, Christ Jesus, who gave Himself for us to redeem us from every lawless deed, and to purify for Himself a people for His own possession, zealous for good deeds. These things speak and exhort and reprove with all authority. Let no one disregard you. (2:11–15)

Don't let anyone move you off the subject of Christ's return. It is the believer's great hope, and the culmination of God's redemptive plan. Nothing is more encouraging and edifying for God's people to discuss with one another. It should be a point of constant conversation until He comes to take us home.

Peter puts it this way: "Prepare your minds for action, keep sober *in spirit*, fix your hope completely on the grace to be brought to you at the revelation of Jesus Christ" (1 Pet. 1:13). We're only waiting on Christ to be revealed. Fix your eyes on Him.

Amid that shocking description of God's coming judgment in Second Peter 3, the apostle included this reminder for us. "Since all these things are to be destroyed in this way, what sort of people ought you to be in holy conduct and godliness . . . Therefore, beloved, since you look for these things, be diligent to be found by Him in peace, spotless and blameless" (3:11, 14).

The hope of Christ's Second Coming should have a sanctifying effect on the church. It should purge believers of worldliness and corruption. We need to live holy lives, knowing that He could return at any moment.

That's what it means to live in light of the Lord's return. If the anticipation of His revelation truly grips our hearts and captivates our minds, it is a source of great comfort and motivation to pursue godliness, holiness, and the sanctification of our conduct, speech, and attitudes. Like Paul said in Titus 2, it should cause "us to deny ungodliness and worldly desires and to live sensibly, righteously and godly in the present age" (2:12). Because when you know He is coming, but not when He's coming, you want to make sure He arrives to find you being the kind of believer you should be, walking faithfully in His likeness.

Christ is coming back. He will return. For the world, it signals divine judgment and flaming retribution. For us, it is the glorious culmination of our salvation, as He comes to deliver us home to His heavenly kingdom. We look forward with eager anticipation of our glorification, and an eternity of perfect fellowship with our Savior.

And in the meantime, we need to follow Paul's instructions to the Colossians. "Set your mind on the things above, not on the things that are on earth. For you have died and your life is hidden with Christ in God. When Christ, who is our life, is revealed, then you also will be revealed with Him in glory" (3:2–4).

Until that great day, we echo John's concluding prayer in Revelation 22:20, "Come, Lord Jesus."

Study Questions:

1. How is the Second Coming of Christ good news for the church and bad news for the world?

2. Why do many Christians avoid eschatology? How might that affect their perspective on the world and their hope of heaven?

3. Knowing what the Lord has promised in terms of future blessings and punishment, how should it affect the way we live?

4. Explain in your own words why the church should look forward to the rapture and how it gives hope to believers.

5. How should the imminence of Christ's return affect your life?

7

What to Look for in a Church, Part 1

How do I find a good church? That's perhaps the most common question I am asked, and I know it reverberates throughout the evangelical world.

Many people outside the church can't find a good church because they don't know what to look for. Ask strangers about the distinguishing marks of a church, and they might point to steeples and stained-glass windows. They might describe the pulpit and the pews, or the parking.

Even those in the church don't seem to know what marks it as a true church. They might cite music and preaching styles or cling to denominational standards. Some make the determination through personal preferences, while others decide on the basis of proximity and convenience.

But none of that is truly definitive or even helpful. It's not up to us to determine what a true church is; God has already defined it in Scripture. And to identify the true church in your area, you need only look to God's Word to see His design for His church. What are the distinguishing marks to look for? What does Scripture tell us about the content of its teaching and the character of its people?

To understand how God designed His church—to see the primary features He expects it to embody—we need to turn our attention to an account from Matthew's gospel, and a powerful exchange between Christ and His disciples.

A Great Confession

First of all, the true church is identified by a great confession. The first thing that marks a faithful, biblical church is what that church confesses to be true. What is the content of its theology? The ordinary church is marked by its doctrine—by one specific point in particular.

We find it as the first point of emphasis in our passage. Matthew wrote, "Now when Jesus came into the district of Caesarea Philippi, He was asking His disciples, 'Who do people say that the Son of Man is?' And they said, 'Some say John the Baptist; and others, Elijah; but still others, Jeremiah, or one of the prophets'" (Matt. 16:13–14). The Jewish people might have had a positive attitude toward Jesus, but they were not willing to acknowledge Him as the Messiah. The disciples' answers reflected the common conversation about who Jesus might be.

"He said to them, 'But who do you say that I am?' Simon Peter answered, 'You are the Christ, the Son of the living God'" (16:15–16). Being the spokesman for the group, Peter spoke up to affirm the disciples' collective confession of Christ's deity. And in verse 18 Jesus said, "Upon this [confession] I will build My church." The great confession of the church is that Jesus is the Messiah, the Son of the living God, who serves as our holy prophet, priest, and King.

The first thing you need to know about a church is its Christology. What does it teach about Jesus Christ? Who do they say He is?

So significant is this issue that the apostle John gave us this stern warning:

> Anyone who goes too far and does not abide in the teaching of Christ, does not have God; the one who abides in the teaching, he has both the Father and the Son. If anyone comes to you and does not bring this teaching, do not receive him into *your* house, and do not give him a greeting; for the one who gives him a greeting participates in his evil deeds. (2 John 9–11)

If somebody corrupts the truth about the person and work of Christ, don't give him or her an audience. Don't even listen to the person's false teaching—turn away and do not participate in his or her corruption. Have nothing to do with those who have nothing to do with the true Christ. It's essentially the negative command of the positive affirmation John made in his first epistle. "We have seen and testify that the Father has sent the Son *to be* the Savior of the world. Whoever confesses that Jesus is the Son of God, God abides in him, and he in God" (1 John 4:14–15).

The true church proclaims Jesus as the Son of God. Paul described the great confession of our faith this way: "If you confess with your mouth Jesus as Lord, and believe in your heart that God raised Him from the dead, you will be saved" (Rom. 10:9). Christ is the foundation of His church (1 Cor. 3:11), the cornerstone of our faith (Eph. 2:20).

We can tolerate no other views of Christ. Paul emphasized the consequences of such corruption. "Even if we, or an angel from heaven, should preach to you a gospel contrary to what we have preached to you, he is to be accursed! As we have said before, so I say again now, if any man is preaching to you a gospel contrary to what you received, he is to be accursed!" (Gal. 1:8–9). Anyone deviating from the biblical truth about Christ is accursed.

We need to have this settled in our minds from the very beginning. None of the other distinguishing marks matter if a church has a wrong view of Christ. The gospels were "written so that you may believe that Jesus is the Christ, the Son of God; and that believing you may have life in His name" (John 20:31). No other acceptable perspective exists. The true church is the body of people who confess the truth about Christ, as revealed in the truth of His Word, without compromise or capitulation.

The true church is about Christ; it's not about you. If you go somewhere that claims to be a true church but all the people ever talk about is you, your life, your needs, and making you happy, that's not a church. They have abandoned their high calling. The church isn't about fixing you—it's about exalting Him; and the people are sanctified by focusing on Him (2 Cor. 3:18).

The Folly of Idolatry

Christ's conversation with His disciples occurred in a providential locale. Under Greek control, it was known as Paneas, named for the Greek god Pan, who was said to have hooves like a goat and reside in a nearby cave. The town was home to a temple dedicated to Pan, along with several other idols to the various Greek and, later, Roman gods. By the time of Christ, as with many ancient cities, the city had been renamed Caesarea Philippi to honor Caesar Augustus. He had a temple there, too.

That meant this town—founded in idolatry and consumed with the worship of idols—was the perfect place for Peter's confession of Christ's deity. There was no better place to declare Jesus as the only true and living Son of God. At the epicenter of idolatry in Israel, where the world's cultures and religions converged, the disciples confessed the uniqueness and exclusivity of Christ. They openly affirmed that all other religions were invalid and unacceptable. They denied that there were multiple pathways to God.

The church today needs to voice the same conviction. In a culture driven and dictated by personal preferences and tolerance, syncretism—people pulling pagan practices into Christianity—abounds. People want "their truth" on their terms. They're convinced they can have what they like of

Jesus and His gospel without excluding anything else. Even some of those who publicly identify with the church have fallen into this worldly, syncretistic mindset—they need to be reminded that it is Christ alone who saves.

The prophet Isaiah exposes the utter foolishness of idol worship.

> Those who fashion a graven image are all of them futile, and their precious things are of no profit; even their own witnesses fail to see or know, so that they will be put to shame. Who has fashioned a god or cast an idol to no profit? Behold, all his companions will be put to shame, for the craftsmen themselves are mere men. Let them all assemble themselves, let them stand up, let them tremble, let them together be put to shame. (Isa. 44:9–11)

Isaiah goes on to describe the various processes that blacksmiths and carpenters employed to shape metal and wood, illustrating how ridiculous it is for people to worship a perishing thing. The prophet even describes the life cycle of a tree—how it has to be planted, watered, and tended to before it ever becomes useful for anything else.

> Then it becomes *something* for a man to burn, so he takes one of them and warms himself; he also makes a fire to bake bread. He also makes a god and worships it; he makes it a graven image and falls down before it. Half of it he burns in the fire; over *this* half he eats meat as he roasts a roast and is satisfied. He also warms himself and says, "Aha! I am warm, I have seen the fire." But the rest of it he makes into a god, his graven image. He falls down before it and worships; he also prays to it and says, "Deliver me, for you are my god." (44:15–17)

Isaiah emphasized the folly of idol worship. It's almost laughable that someone would pray for deliverance to a god they fashioned with their own hands. But such is the tragic blindness of false religion. In fact, Isaiah said that such spiritual blindness is part of God's judgment.

> They do not know, nor do they understand, for He has smeared over their eyes so that they cannot see and their hearts so that they cannot comprehend. No one recalls, nor is there knowledge or understanding to say, "I have burned half of it in the fire and also have baked bread over its coals. I roast meat and eat *it*. Then I make the rest of it into an abomination, I fall down before a block of wood!" (44:18–19).

Idolatry pervades society today just as it did in the ancient world. The main difference is that the gods aren't made of wood, stone, and iron anymore. Today, the culture kneels before the idol of self-love.

Our Common Confession

Peter made a further affirmation of Christ's exclusivity in John 6. After another mass departure of His followers, Jesus asked His disciples, "'You do not want to go away also, do you?' Simon Peter answered Him, 'Lord, to whom shall we go? You have words of eternal life. We have believed and have come to know that You are the Holy One of God'" (6:67–69). That is the confession that identifies a true believer and a true church—it is the assembly of those who confess the truth about Christ.

The church is not a group of people who need a motivational talk. It's not for people who want to manage their addictions or who are looking for a bump in their self-esteem. It's not a weekly venue for you to network with potential customers or clients. It's not a place where you mindlessly go through rituals and rites.

Someone once described the church like a carousel—a lot of music and a lot of ups and downs, but you get off exactly where you got on. And certainly many places that claim to be churches are like that.

But the true church is the assembly of those who make the greatest of all confessions: that Jesus is Lord.

Writing after Christ's earthly work was complete, Paul spelled out the church's great confession in full. "By common confession"—which is to say, this is the common confession of true believers—"great is the mystery of godliness: He who was revealed in the flesh, was vindicated in the Spirit, seen by angels, proclaimed among the nations, believed on in the world, taken up in glory" (1 Tim. 3:16).

No doubt this was a hymn in the early church. With just six third-person, singular, aorist verbs with rhythm and parallelism, Paul provided us with a minimalist, yet comprehensive, look at the person and work of Christ. "Revealed in the flesh" speaks to His incarnation. He was "vindicated in the Spirit"—that is, He was declared righteous by the Spirit, who worked through Him throughout His life and ministry. Christ was "seen by angels" at His birth, through His temptation, and at His resurrection. And when His earthly ministry was complete, He was "taken up in glory." And from that day to today, He has been "proclaimed among the nations" and "believed on in the world." This is the church's unanimous, triumphant confession: Jesus Christ is the Son of the living God. He is Lord. He is Redeemer.

The church is not merely a place or group that focuses on the sentimentalism or sacramentalism about a man named Jesus. It's the body of transformed lives—men and women living in union with Christ by the miracle of regeneration. We have been transferred from death to life, and we are joined with Christ in one spirit. We confess Him as Lord and Savior. He is the Son of God. The church is the gathering of people who echo Peter: Where else could we go? Christ alone has the words of life and salvation.

And because of this common confession, everything in the true church is Christ-centered. Everything is Christ-focused and Christ-magnifying. It's not about the people. In the true church, people are not there for themselves. They're there to exalt Christ—to glorify and honor His name. As Paul put it, "We are the *true* circumcision, who worship in the Spirit of God and glory in Christ Jesus and put no confidence in the flesh" (Phil. 3:3).

A Great Communication

The true church is first identified by its great confession of the truth about Christ. That's the foundation. But there is a second distinguishing mark—a sub-foundation, if you will. Under the foundation sits a pillar of truth, to borrow Paul's analogy. The true church is marked by a great confession that is undergirded by a great *communication.*

If the true church is going to confess Jesus as Lord, where do we receive the truth that brings about that confession? Where does our conviction come from? We return to Christ's conversation with His disciples in Matthew 16. In verse 16 Peter confessed the deity of Christ. The Lord responded in verse 17, "Blessed are you, Simon Barjona, because flesh and blood did not reveal this to you, but My Father who is in heaven."

The true knowledge of Christ does not come through human reason or intuition. It isn't derived from some scientific methodology. It's not the product of man's intellectual pursuit. The revelation of the truth about Christ comes from heaven alone. The Son is revealed by the Father. Peter made his confession because God communicated the truth to him from heaven.

The Lord said to Peter, "You didn't come up with this on your own. This didn't come to you by any flesh-and-blood means"—that is, any human means. There is no human source of this saving confession. Paul affirmed the same truth in Galatians 1:11–12, "I would have you know, brethren, that the gospel which was preached by me is not according to man. For I neither received it from man, nor was I taught it, but *I received it* through a revelation of Jesus Christ."

The truth about Christ, the gospel, is God's revelation. And it's His only written revelation. All other supposed religions spring out of man's corrupt imagination, or from demons (1 Tim. 4:1).

God is not a God of contradictions. His revelation of His Son is the truth, and anything else that claims to be from Him—and especially anything that contradicts the revelation of His Son—is a lie.

How did the Father reveal to Peter the truth concerning Christ? Through Christ Himself in the Incarnation. Peter didn't have the New Testament, but God revealed Himself through the person of Jesus Christ. Peter and the other disciples were uniquely able to know God and His revealed truth through the Word incarnate.

We might be inclined to be jealous. We might say, "Wouldn't it have been great to be alive at the time of Christ—to see Him up close and in person?" But Peter himself tells us not to think like that. In his second epistle, he wrote about being an eyewitness to the Lord.

> We did not follow cleverly devised tales when we made known to you the power and coming of our Lord Jesus Christ, but we were eyewitnesses of His majesty. For when He received honor and glory from God the Father, such an utterance as this was made to Him by the Majestic Glory, "This is My beloved Son with whom I am well-pleased"—and we ourselves heard this utterance made from heaven when we were with Him on the holy mountain. (2 Pet. 1:16–18)

However, he said to his readers, "We have the prophetic word *made* more sure, to which you do well to pay attention to as to a lamp shining in a dark place, until the day dawns and the morning star arises in your hearts" (1:19). We have the "word *made* more sure." We have the better part.

If we had witnessed the life of Christ, we would only know what we experienced firsthand; we wouldn't have the full and comprehensive truth of Him provided to us in the four gospel accounts, or the preaching of His eyewitnesses contained in Acts, the epistles, and Revelation. We have so much more than we could have ever seen with our own eyes through the Holy Spirit-inspired New Testament record (2 Pet. 1:21). We have everything God wants us to know about Christ's life and the fullness of His ministry.

We have the truth—God's great communication to us about His Son. Through this truth we have been born again (1 Pet. 1:23). Through it we are sanctified (John 17:17). And through it we grow in the likeness of our Savior (Eph. 4:15). God's truth is the foundation for the life of the church. And you'll know that you're in a true church because it is focused on exalting Christ and proclaiming the saving, transforming, and sanctifying Scripture that reveals Him.

WHAT IS THE "ROCK" ON WHICH CHRIST IS BUILDING?

Christ's affirming words for Peter's confession continued. "I also say to you that you are Peter, and upon this rock I will build my church; and the gates of Hades will not overpower it" (Matt. 16:18). We've already considered the fact that Christ alone is building His church and that no weapon of Satan can overcome it.

But the beginning of verse 18 is a point of much misunderstanding and controversy. In fact, you could say that it has unleashed deception on earth through the heresies of the Roman Catholic Church. Catholics hinge their false claims of papal authority on their misinterpretation of this verse, arguing that Christ was identifying Peter as the first pope of the church. They've turned the Lord's words inside out and upside-down, and through their self-serving interpretation, they have failed to build the true church of Christ.

What was Jesus actually saying? His point was not to inaugurate Peter as pope, but, to play on words, that would emphasize the magnitude of his confession.

Peter's name comes from a Greek word (petros) that means "small stone." The word translated "rock" is petra, which refers to vast boulders and mountain peaks. Jesus was emphasizing the contrast. Peter was just a man—a small stone, in the grand scheme of things. But his confession of Jesus as Lord was substantial—it was the massive and sturdy rock bed Christ would build His church on.

The rock is the revelation from the Father in heaven regarding the Lord Jesus Christ. It's the gospel. The church is built upon the revelation bestowed by God through Christ onto the apostles. Through the inspiration of the Holy Spirit, they handed down that revelation to us, and it remains permanently the only foundation of God's true church.

The church isn't built on Peter or any other sinful man. He was no pope or king for the church. As we'll see later in this passage, it was almost no time at all before Christ had to confront Peter as an emissary of Satan. And we know that he would go on to deny Christ in the hours before the Crucifixion. By God's grace, he would mature into a faithful preacher and apostle to shepherd the early church. He became a godly leader and a martyr for the truth. But he was just a man—a small pebble compared to the bedrock of divine revelation.

The Word has the ultimate authority in the church. That's why, as we've already seen, the early church was devoted to the study of the apostles' teaching (Acts 2:42). It's why Jude instructed his readers, "You, beloved, ought to remember the words that were spoken beforehand by the apostles of our Lord Jesus Christ" (2:17). In other words, turn away from false teachers and get back to the words you received from the apostles.

That is the gift that has been handed down to God's people through church history. God revealed His truth through the incarnation of His Son (Heb. 1:1). And after Christ had returned to glory, the Father revealed His truth through the inspiration of the Holy Spirit (2 Tim. 3:16; 2 Pet. 1:21), leading His chosen men to write down everything that Christ had done and record the early preaching of the cross in the first-century church. Nothing is left for us to unearth or decode—no mysteries that need solving. Through His power, we have His complete revelation.

In fact, what we have in the pages of the New Testament is as true and pure and divine and heavenly and accurate a presentation and revelation of Jesus Christ as was the Incarnation itself. That's a remarkable statement to consider, but it's true. It has to be, if we're begotten and sanctified by the word that is written. It has to be as true, as complete, and as powerful as the revelation of God in the very person of Christ because it is the foundation for the building of Christ's church.

We're not built on Peter, the apostles, or any succession of popes. Only God's revelation of His Son through the pages of Scripture provides the strong and reliable rock bed sufficient to be the foundation of His church.

The Keys to the Kingdom

Returning to our passage, we find another frequently misunderstood verse that merits discussion. Matthew 16:19 continues Christ's commending words, "I will give you the keys of the kingdom of heaven; and whatever you bind on earth shall have been bound in heaven, and whatever you loose on earth shall have been loosed in heaven." This is an interesting statement.

In order to get the keys to anything you have to be trustworthy. Keys indicate access and authority. But what are the keys Christ referred to? We know they aren't the supremacy of some pope. We know it's not authority or power for some cardinal, bishop, priest, or any other religious leader to wield. It's not bestowed on some special class of believers. This is a gift entrusted to all believers—every Christian has these keys.

He's talking about the revelation of the Father concerning the Son. He's talking about the gospel. Every believer who understands the truth about Christ enough to believe it and be saved possesses the keys to the kingdom of heaven. It's an amazing privilege that the Lord has entrusted to all of us. You and I can go into the world and preach the gospel. We can fulfill the Great Commission. You might think you're somehow inadequate, but you have the keys to the kingdom of heaven. What else do you need?

Moreover, heaven is in perfect agreement with us when we faithfully use the keys to the kingdom. As Christ said in verse 19, "Whatever you bind on earth shall have been bound in heaven, and whatever you loose on earth shall have been loosed in heaven."

Again, that's not referring to some special privileges reserved for elite believers. It doesn't mean that you have authority to forgive or condemn. We don't absolve each other of sin or sit in judgment.

Rather, Christ referred to an old rabbinical idea. The rabbis would say to someone who was not repentant, "You are bound in your sin." Likewise, they would affirm repentant sinners, saying, "You are loosed from your sin." They weren't making judgments of their own but simply reflecting what God had said.

That's exactly what we do. Based on people's response to the gospel, we can tell whether they are still bound in their sins or that they have been set free from them. If somebody rejects the gospel, I can say with certainty that he is still bound in his sin. But if he accepts the gospel and repents, I can rejoice with him that he has been set free from sin's bondage. And in either instance, what I say has already been confirmed in heaven because I'm simply applying the Word that came from heaven. We have the keys to the kingdom of heaven, the gospel that opens the door to all who believe.

Note that the keys to the kingdom don't involve our creativity or ingenuity. We can't do anything to make them more powerful. We don't attempt to usher people into God's kingdom by appealing to their fleshly desires or felt needs. We can't entertain anyone into the kingdom—the best that can produce is a superficial response that leads to false assurance. As Paul wrote, "Faith *comes* from hearing, and hearing by the word of Christ" (Rom. 10:17).

Heaven's kingdom has no other key. As we teach and preach the truth of God's Word and the gospel of our Lord Jesus Christ, the Father in heaven reveals the truth to the hearts of men and women and brings them to true saving faith.

God graciously allows us to participate in the work of His Word, inviting all who will come by faith to enter His kingdom.

SHEPHERD THE FLOCK

In his epistle to the Ephesians, Paul highlighted the work of evangelism, along with some other specific roles God called His servants to in the administration of His Word. God "gave some *as* apostles, and some *as* prophets, and some *as* evangelists, and some *as* pastors and teachers" (Eph. 4:11). The aim for all who serve in those roles is the same: "For the equipping of the saints for the work of service, to the building up of the body of Christ; until we all attain to the unity of the faith, and of the knowledge of the Son of God, to a mature man, to the measure of the stature which belongs to the fullness of Christ" (4:12–13).

The work of the Word doesn't end with leading people to the kingdom. God has given us His great communication for the building up of believers. And He has set aside His men to shepherd the flock.

That was the very task the Lord spelled out for Peter by the Sea of Galilee after the Resurrection. Confirming Peter's love for Him, Christ charged the disciple three times with the care of His flock: "Tend My lambs" (John 21:15), "shepherd My sheep" (21:16), and "tend My sheep" (21:17).

In his first epistle, Peter passed along the same instructions to the leaders in the churches he wrote to: "Shepherd the flock of God among you" (1 Pet. 5:2). The church is the flock of God—the redeemed He has called out of darkness—who confess Jesus as Lord and live under the authority of His Word, by which they have been saved and sanctified. And for God's chosen men, their job is to shepherd His flock—to guide, feed, nurture, and protect His sheep.

Many today pretend to be shepherds, but they have no love for the sheep. They don't lead them carefully or look out for those who might be prone to wandering away. They don't give any thought to their spiritual nutrition, leaving them to eat whatever they can find on their own. They don't protect the sheep from the various threats that surround them. In fact, these false shepherds—these hirelings—routinely neglect God's sheep. Many only seem interested in entertaining goats.

But for true shepherds, there is no greater responsibility. They love the sheep and give their lives for their sake. They faithfully feed God's people the rich nourishment of His Word and lead them to grow in Christlikeness. And they faithfully protect them. Speaking to the elders of the Ephesian church, Paul urged:

> Be on guard for yourselves and for all the flock, among which the Holy Spirit has made you overseers, to shepherd the church of God which He

> purchased with His own blood. I know that after my departure savage wolves will come in among you, not sparing the flock; and from among your own selves men will arise, speaking perverse things, to draw away the disciples after them. Therefore be on the alert, remembering that night and day for a period of three years I did not cease to admonish each one with tears. And now I commend you to God and to the word of His grace, which is able to build *you* up. (Acts 20:28–32)

The instrument of the shepherd's work—the feeding, nurturing, and protecting of God's sheep—is the Word of God. His revelation of divine truth is their richest food, their greatest comfort, and their strongest defense.

I've heard some pastors of so-called churches say they don't believe in expositing the Bible because nonbelievers aren't interested in that or because they want something more "relevant" for their people. So they exegete movies and television. They let pop culture dictate the diet of the sheep, and then wonder why they're starving, malnourished, and not growing. They've ignored the testimony of the Chief Shepherd, who prayed for those under His care, "Sanctify them in the truth; Your word is truth" (John 17:17).

Scripture is the single supernatural, indispensable agent that saves and sanctifies. We are begotten by the word of truth, and transformed by it into the likeness of Christ. It is our only source of true spiritual food—the only nourishment that promotes true growth. It is the only food that a shepherd should give to his flock and the only means through which he can protect and lead them.

If you're looking for a church, consider many distinguishing marks—we'll see several more in the next chapter. But if it's not an assembly of people who make the great confession that Jesus is Lord, and who come under the authority of the great communication of the Word of God, it's not a true church.

Study Questions:

1. Explain in your own words how a church might talk a lot about Jesus without making the great confession of His deity.

2. What are some examples of syncretism in the church today? Where do you see the worship of God compromised and corrupted by the worship of self?

3. What is the danger of a church that is designed to appeal to the interests of unbelievers?

4. Explain in your own words why Roman Catholics are wrong to defend the papacy from Matthew 16:18, and what Jesus actually meant when He referred to "this rock."

5. How did Peter come to know the truth about Christ? What implications does that have for the church today?

8

What to Look for in a Church, Part 2

CONFUSION ABOUNDS today across the evangelical landscape regarding what the church is and what it is supposed to be. But this confusion is unnecessary. God has been very clear about His design for His church.

God's church is called to be faithful, not fashionable. It's called to be persecuted, not popular. It's called to be a force for salvation, not social change. It's called to declare the truth in love, not deceptive tolerance and unity in a lie. It's not to be known by its novelty or uniqueness, but by its consistency and commonality.

It's no badge of honor for a church to claim it's not like any other church. Rather, the true church should be proud to say that it's like every other church that follows and adheres to the prescriptions of Scripture.

In short, the Lord's church is to be marked by biblical fidelity.

To understand what that looks like practically, we've been examining a passage from Matthew's gospel in which Christ spelled out some of the key features and distinguishing marks of His true church. In our previous chapter, we saw that the ordinary, biblical church is marked first by a great confession—that Jesus is Lord (Matt. 16:13–16), and that our confession is revealed through a great communication (16:17–19), in the form of God's revelation in His Word. That brings us to a third characteristic of God's church.

A Great Contrast

The true church is marked by a great contrast. Matthew 16:20 tells us, "Then He warned the disciples that they should tell no one that He was the Christ."

This strikes the reader as a surprising statement, in light of everything that had just been affirmed about Peter's confession. It seems counterintuitive, as though Christ were issuing the opposite of the Great Commission.

But don't get carried away with such thoughts. Remember that at this point, the gospel had not yet been fully revealed because Christ had not yet been crucified. He hadn't yet risen from the dead. And the Holy Spirit had not yet come to indwell believers and empower the preaching of the gospel. So this isn't truly tantamount to a reversal of the Great Commission.

Still, it is a strong prohibition from the Lord. He was not merely asking them to tone it down a little or back off a bit. It's not a suggestion to simply slow down. He was telling them, "Don't do this at all. Don't tell people I am the Messiah. Don't tell anyone."

So how do we make sense of this stern restriction?

To understand Christ's instructions, we need to remember how the first-century Jews perceived the promised Messiah. In John 6, after Jesus fed the massive crowd of people who had gathered to hear Him teach, Scripture records their reaction. Verse 14 says, "Therefore when the people saw the sign which He had performed, they said, 'This is truly the Prophet who is to come into the world.'"

The Jews were looking for a Messiah who would eliminate all of their enemies and solve all their problems. They expected a leader to provide peace and safety. They were looking for security and prosperity in this life. They were looking for the one who would bring to pass the promises of the Abrahamic covenant, the Davidic covenant, and all of the prophets God raised up through the centuries.

Jesus feeding that crowd of about 20,000 had the potential to play right into their false ideas of Messiah. They were ready to have their enemies wiped out and to ascend to the top of the social ladder. They were tired of their hardscrabble lives; they were ready for ease and comfort. This crowd thought they had found the one who could provide all that, so they were ready to inaugurate His reign.

But John noted us how Christ responded to this notion. "So Jesus, perceiving that they were intending to come and take Him by force to make Him king, withdrew again to the mountain by Himself alone" (6:15). They saw Him as the ultimate human ruler, God's anointed, who was to be their king. Their perspectives were political, social, material, and military.

In His first coming, Christ didn't come to do any of that. On those few occasions when He created food, He did it to demonstrate His deity. That's also why He effectively banished sickness and disease from the nation during His public ministry—to show that He was God incarnate and to give people a foretaste of His kingdom, which would provide an abundance of food, health, and prosperity. But He did not come the first time to establish an earthly kingdom.

The true church presents a great contrast to what the world is pursuing. It presents a kingdom that is not of this world.

Not of This World

John 18:33 says, "Pilate entered again into the Praetorium, and summoned Jesus and said to Him, 'Are You the King of the Jews?'"

In reality, He wasn't the king they were looking for. They briefly thought He was, but they ultimately rejected Him because He didn't fulfill their expectations. He disappointed them. And their disappointment was profound for two reasons. First, He did not overthrow their enemies and free them from Roman occupation. But secondly, when He did attack, He attacked them and their false religion. He pointed out their hypocrisy. So they rejected Him as Messiah and handed Him over for execution.

His kingdom was not the one they were expecting. Jesus made that point in His reply to Pilate. "My kingdom is not of this world. If My kingdom were of this world, then My servants would be fighting so that I would not be handed over to the Jews; but as it is, My kingdom is not of this realm" (18:36). A time will come in the future when His kingdom will be of this world, and He won't need any help establishing it.

"Pilate said to Him, 'So You are a king?' Jesus answered, 'You say correctly that I am a king. For this I have been born, and for this I have come into the world, to testify to the truth. Everyone who is of the truth hears My voice'" (18:37). Christ did not come to establish His kingdom on earth at that time, but to preach the truth that is essential to the spiritual kingdom and to do the saving work necessary to make kingdom citizens.

We need to draw an important point out of Christ's words. The church is the spiritual kingdom of Christ on earth today, and it has nothing to do with earthly kingdoms. As He said, "My kingdom"—the church—"is not of this world." So we don't fight to advance His kingdom. We don't overthrow governments or seize land in the name of Christ's kingdom. Throughout history, terrible wars and bloody conflicts were fought, supposedly in the name of the church. But God's people don't do that. Heaven's kingdom does not advance at the tip of a sword.

The kingdom we belong to is not part of this world. It is transcendent. It's separate and alien. It's spiritual, independent of this temporal world and its powers. We understand that the kingdom of heaven has no connection to the kingdoms of this world.

Many of the Reformers didn't share that view. They decided that since there were Catholic countries like Italy and France, they should establish Protestant nations out of the Reformation. Countries like Germany, Switzerland, and England all became institutionally Christian nations. And they would go to war with Catholic nations, all in the name of advancing Christ's kingdom, while ignoring the clear words of Christ that His kingdom does not advance through those means.

Here's a simple way to think of it—it is utterly irrelevant to the kingdom of heaven what happens in any earthly kingdom. It has nothing to do with the building of Christ's kingdom. So we reject the notion of national religion. We reject a sacral society. The mandate is to advance the kingdom one salvation at a time, through the preaching of the gospel, not political might.

Now, that doesn't mean we should withdraw from society altogether. We still need to be good citizens. We need to love our neighbors as ourselves (Mark 12:31) and live peaceable lives (Rom. 12:18). And when given the opportunity, we want to influence the powers that be and exercise our vote to elect leaders and establish laws that reflect God's will for His creation. We want to be an influence for good in the world as much as possible.

But none of that is the mission of the church. We don't worry about rearranging the deck chairs on the Titanic—we know there is no point. Our focus is getting people into the lifeboats before the ship sinks. That's what the true church does.

It's incredible how much time, money, and effort professing believers and churches put into making incremental improvements to Satan's kingdom. In recent generations, several church groups and denominations became so consumed with social issues and establishing morality that they abandoned the gospel altogether. They gave themselves over to social activism and cultural conquest, failing to understand that they were making superficial changes at best.

Immorality damns, but so can morality. No external changes can accomplish the regenerating, transforming work of the Spirit through His Word.

The world desperately wants the church to abandon the proclamation of the gospel and the exaltation of Christ and get caught up in social issues instead. That serves Satan's purpose. Turning the church into an agency of social welfare and moral influence is his strategy. He would love for us to become entangled in cultural conflicts and temporal concerns. He wants our focus on the deck chairs, not the lifeboats.

But we do not exist to promote Judeo-Christian ethics. We're not concerned with institutionalizing morality and behavior modification. Our mission is not better government institutions or agencies. It's not better laws or higher standards. Our mission is better people, transformed through the gospel.

And the gospel so thoroughly transforms people that they will have a transforming, sanctifying influence on society. That's the only hope for truly ending sexual sin, racism, crime, or any of the countless corrupting influences in our culture—the gospel of Jesus Christ is the only power that makes an eternal difference. Let the world bear witness to the transformed lives of those who belong to heaven's kingdom.

A Great Conquest

Christ's exchange with His disciples in Matthew 16 presents a fourth feature of the church. Verse 21 says, "From that time Jesus began to show His disciples that He must go to Jerusalem, and suffer many things from the elders and chief priests and scribes, and be killed, and be raised up on the third day." The parallel passage in Mark's gospel says, "He was stating the matter plainly" (Mark 8:32). What we see here is that the true church acknowledges a great conquest.

The church is a triumphant reality. That doesn't mean we have conquered lands or people groups. As we've just seen, our mission has nothing to do with earthly kingdoms or social change. Rather, we have triumphed in Christ. In the words of Paul, "Thanks be to God, who always leads us in triumph in Christ" (2 Cor. 2:14). Our Savior has conquered the greatest enemy of all enemies.

And what is that enemy? Sin. Through His death and resurrection, Christ has conquered sin and its penalty—death. He has set us free from the slavery of sin and the fear of death, making us citizens of His kingdom. The great conquest of the church is the cross. His victory is the good news proclaimed by the church.

He told the disciples that He was going to "be killed, and be raised up on the third day" (Matt. 16:21). In dying, He conquered sin, and in rising, He conquered death. That great conquest defines the church—the fact that we are no longer under the power of sin and death. We have a Savior who has set us free from both.

You don't hear that message in many so-called churches today. To listen to them, you would think the great proclamation of the church had to do with social advancement, building self-esteem, acquiring wealth, or wish fulfillment. They preach a message of satisfaction in the here and now—one that appeals to the desires of the unregenerate world.

The prosperity gospel is perhaps the best example of Satan's success in clouding and confusing Christ's purpose for His people. Millions around the globe today are caught up in churches that, to one degree or another, promote the lies of the prosperity gospel—which is truly no *gospel* at all. It doesn't set anyone free. It's merely another form of bondage to this world with its wicked, selfish whims.

To start, the prosperity gospel embodies blasphemous irreverence toward the Trinity. It views God the Father as your servant or slave, waiting in the wings until you speak Him into power through your words—most often in the form of presumptuous demands.

Very little emphasis is given to Christ. His life and ministry, and even His sacrificial death and triumphant resurrection all become somewhat superfluous when you can order the Father around with the power of your words. And despite frequent mentions of the Holy Spirit, there is little emphasis toward dependence on Him, since all the power to command God resides in you. Such warped theology turns the Creator God of the universe into a wish-fulfilling genie, and puts the focus of the church onto the pursuit of everything the unregenerate world wants: health and wealth.

The prosperity gospel plays to the basest desires of the human heart. It's a false gospel of selfishness and greed, an attempt to sanctify and validate what should be mortified. It perverts God's plan of redemption and substitutes the sinner's wicked, worldly desires for His will.

That obsession with temporal riches and rewards brushes aside the great conquest of Christ. It relegates His sacrifice and His victory over sin and death to little more than a footnote. It makes no sense that many of these churches still have crosses prominently displayed—a pot of gold would be far more consistent with their emphasis.

The gospel of Christ and the true church don't offer that. We don't offer miracle healings. We don't offer material riches and wealth. We don't offer cheap psychology or boosted self-esteem. We don't offer anything that unregenerate people want. In fact, we offer only what unregenerate people *don't* want: self-denial and the elimination of their sin. Through Christ's triumph on the cross, we offer forgiveness of sin and eternal life in the glory of heaven. We offer a Savior who "bore our sins in His body on the cross, so that we might die to sin and live to righteousness" (1 Pet. 2:24); the One "who knew no sin [was made] *to be* sin on our behalf, so that we might become the righteousness of God in Him" (2 Cor. 5:21).

In Romans 6, Paul described Christ's conquest of both the cross and the grave, and the implications for His people.

> We have been buried with Him through baptism into death, so that as Christ was raised from the dead through the glory of the Father, so we too might walk in newness of life. For if we have become united with *Him* in the likeness of His death, certainly we shall also be *in the likeness* of His resurrection, knowing this, that our old self was crucified with *Him*, in order that our body of sin might be done away with, so that we would no longer be slaves to sin; for he who has died is freed from sin.
>
> Now if we have died with Christ, we believe that we shall also live with Him, knowing that Christ, having been raised from the dead, is never to die again; death no longer is master over Him. For the death that He died, He died to sin once for all; but the life that He lives, He lives to God. Even so consider yourselves to be dead to sin, but alive to God in Christ Jesus. (Rom. 6:4–11)

You don't find anything there about health and happiness in this fleeting life. Christ didn't suffer the agonies of the cross to make you rich; He didn't rise from the dead to fulfill your hopes and dreams.

The Lord's conquest over the cross and the grave was to purchase a people for Himself for eternity. The triumph was breaking our bondage to sin and setting us free from the fear of death into eternal life.

The Focal Point of History

The true church offers the great conquest of Christ—the glorious purpose for which God providentially orchestrated thousands of years of world history and through which He continues to build His church.

Do you understand the magnitude of that? History has no other goal than the gathering of God's chosen and redeemed people into eternity to glorify Him forever. The church is why He created the universe. It's why He formed the earth and breathed life into humanity. The saving, sanctifying, and glorifying of His church is the reason the universe exists. Our finite minds can barely comprehend it.

Here's one way to put it into perspective. If you go back through human history, you see a series of great civilizations and empires. Egypt and Babylon stand out in the early parts of the Old Testament. We think of the Medo-Persian Empire, the great Greek Empire, and the Roman Empire that dominated during the time of Christ. Several modern nations were once home to great global empires—China, Russia, England. You might even consider the United States as a kind of empire, wielding influence all over the globe.

But none of them dominates human history. The great and lasting empire is the church. Those empires have all come and gone, and others will continue to come and go as long as the Lord tarries. But the church endures forever. It will continue to be built until it is complete, and then it will be gathered into glory for eternity.

That is Christ's great conquest. It's not the conquest of some temporal discomfort but His triumph over sin and death and hell through both His cross and His empty tomb. And by His death and resurrection, He provides us with the forgiveness of our sins and a righteous standing before God. He bestows on us a transformed life filled with love, joy, peace, gentleness, goodness, faith, meekness, and self-control. And He promises us an eternity with Him in heaven, and a host of lavish glories and blessings that human language can't even fully describe.

Christ's triumph over sin and death is the focal point of human history, as He builds His church through His great conquest.

A Great Conflict

From our vantage point in church history, we can look back at Christ's death and resurrection and immediately see their necessity and importance for the building of His church. But Peter didn't have the same perspective, and his response to the news of the Lord's impending death illustrates for us another distinguishing mark of the true church: a great conflict.

Matthew recorded, "Peter took Him aside and began to rebuke Him, saying, 'God forbid *it*, Lord! This shall never happen to You'" (Matt. 16:22). Peter impetuously pulled aside the Creator of the universe to have a private word and set Him straight.

Matthew says he "began to rebuke Him"—this wasn't a brief confrontation. It wasn't a simple, isolated statement. Peter kept it up; he was berating the Lord about the idea of His death. He rejected the notion that Christ would be killed, and he rebuked the Lord for even suggesting it.

He even went so far as to say, "God forbid it, Lord!" The irony of that statement was lost on Peter. He was pleading with the Lord to forbid and forestall something that He had just said was going to happen. You can see here that the false expectations about Messiah had permeated the minds of even the disciples. Peter was basically saying, "You can't die; that doesn't fit with the plan."

The Lord quickly stifled Peter's shortsighted complaint. "He turned and said to Peter, 'Get behind Me, Satan! You are a stumbling block to Me; for you are not setting your mind on God's interests, but man's'" (16:23).

Anything contrary to God's will puts you on Satan's side and aligns you with his demonic cause. Christ used this strong language to arrest Peter's attention and put him back into alignment with God's interests.

Many churches today likewise need to be shocked back into alignment with God's will. His interests and priorities must set the program for the church, not those of humans. A church aligned to human interests is immature, irreverent, and carnal.

You can find churches fitting that description all over—their pervasive influence is the reason so much confusion exists about what the church is supposed to be. On the other hand, a church aligned with God's interests will be bound to His Word, devoted to His worship, and faithfully growing in the likeness of His Son.

We're at war with Satan. We're battling his interests and his ideologies. The church is caught up in the great conflict between the will of the devil and the will of God.

Satan is the ruler of this world; he is "the prince of the power of the air" (Eph. 2:2). Christ referred to him as "a murderer from the beginning" who "does not stand in the truth because there is no truth in him" (John 8:44).

In the same statement, the Lord identified the unregenerate as the offspring of the devil. And as God's children, we are involved in the ancient conflict between our Father and Satan.

Paul reminds us, "Our struggle is not against flesh and blood, but against the rulers, against the powers, against the world forces of this darkness, against the spiritual *forces* of wickedness in the heavenly *places*" (Eph. 6:12).

Our war is not against the unregenerate—they are the mission field. Rather, our war is with Satan and demons that manipulate the rulers and the powers of this world toward demonic, corrupt desires. Remember, "the weapons of our warfare are not of the flesh, but divinely powerful for the destruction of fortresses. *We are* destroying speculations and every lofty thing raised up against the knowledge of God, and *we are* taking every thought captive to the obedience of Christ" (2 Cor. 10:4–5).

We're battling unbiblical ideologies and false teaching—anything that stands opposed to the will and the Word of God. We're fighting against everything that opposes His interests.

And as Peter illustrated, that can occasionally include believers. Christ referred to him as "a stumbling block" (Matt. 16:23). While he had no intention of openly rebelling against God, he was acting as an obstruction to the Lord's divine purposes. In his ignorant zeal, he had set himself in opposition to God.

We can identify plenty of obvious stumbling blocks that the world erects to fight God and His will. All the false forms of Christianity that twist and pervert Scripture are satanic stumbling blocks. All other man-made religions would be as well. And we can identify plenty of other unbiblical worldviews and ideologies that are diametrically opposed to the purposes of God.

But we can also find many stumbling blocks to God's interests inside the church—most of them far less obvious. Ignorance of God's truth—and any teaching that propagates ignorance—is a stumbling block, as it impedes discernment and spiritual growth. Any misrepresentation of God, Christ, the Holy Spirit, or the Bible would qualify as a stumbling block that perverts and corrupts God's truth.

Human-centered hermeneutics and sentimental theology leading to the misinterpretation of the Bible are likewise stumbling blocks when it comes to God's purposes for His church. Any time the church is not confronting evil but compromising with it—that is clearly in opposition to the Lord's interests.

False teachers abound in the church today. It's very easy to find a building and draw a crowd, to set yourself up as a church without ever meeting any of the biblical qualifications or evidencing the distinguishing marks of a true church. People do it all the time. And we know that Satan sows tares in the midst of the church (Matt. 13:25). Recall Paul's warning to the elders at the Ephesian church that "savage wolves will come in among you, not sparing the flock; and from among your own selves men will arise, speaking perverse things, to draw away the disciples after them. Therefore be on the alert" (Acts 20:29–31).

We have to be aware of all the stumbling blocks—those presented by the world, and those in our midst—in the great conflict against Satan.

That's why I'm so passionate about biblical education and faithfully training people for ministry. At The Master's Seminary and The Master's

University, we emphasize the necessity of biblical fidelity and sound doctrine. The Lord wants a pure church—both in practice and in doctrine. We need people who fully understand the will of God, as revealed in Scripture, to lead in the church, rather than people who are carelessly obstructing the very purpose for which it exists.

You could think of it this way: You don't want to find yourself at a church that seems to be at peace with the world, where they don't perceive the conflict or understand their role in it. But when you find a body of believers that understands the great conflict and is vigorously engaged in the battle for the truth, you've found a true church.

A Great Contradiction

Extending from the church's great conflict, we see another of its features: a great contradiction. Our conflict with the world leads to a life lived in contradiction to its pursuits and priorities.

After He rebuked Peter's impetuous words, the Lord turned to issue a warning to the rest of His men about what it would mean to truly follow Him.

> Jesus said to His disciples, "If anyone wishes to come after Me, he must deny himself, and take up his cross and follow Me. For whoever wishes to save his life will lose it; but whoever loses his life for My sake will find it. For what will it profit a man if he gains the whole world and forfeits his soul? Or what will a man give in exchange for his soul?" (Matt. 16:24–26)

The Christian life is not about self-fulfillment or personal achievement. It's the opposite of that. It's the opposite of every warped promise that so-called churches make today regarding health and wealth, about happiness and satisfaction in this life. They invite people to join them so they can have everything they want. But that is an unbiblical deception.

In reality, according to Christ Himself, the Christian life is about self-denial—completely dying to self for the work of the kingdom and the exaltation of our Savior. It's a life of self-sacrifice for the sake of the gospel. It's the embodiment of John the Baptist's words about Christ: "He must increase, but I must decrease" (John 3:30). One Puritan writer put it this way:

> Lord, high and holy, meek and lowly, let me learn by paradox that the way down is the way up, that to be low is to be high, that the broken heart is the healed heart, that the contrite spirit is the rejoicing spirit, that the repenting soul is the victorious soul, that to have nothing is to possess everything, that to bear the cross is to wear the crown, that to give is to receive. Let

> me find thy light in my darkness, thy joy in my sorrow, thy grace in my sin, thy riches in my poverty, thy glory in my valley, thy life in my death.[1]

What greater contradiction could there be to how the world lives and operates?

Describing the believer's life of self-sacrifice, Christ presented three conditions. "If anyone wishes to come after Me, he must deny himself" (Matt. 16:24). The verb here means, "to disown or disassociate." It's not merely that you cut ties with the world to follow Christ—you must also abandon the "you" that you once were. You plead with the Lord to deliver you from yourself. It's denying everything that is natural, depraved, fleshly, and sinful about yourself. You surrender your dreams, desires, and personal pursuits. All your ambitions and efforts must be surrendered to Christ. That is true conversion: The self is completely cast aside.

Christ described this attitude in the Beatitudes. "Blessed are the poor in spirit, for theirs is the kingdom of heaven. Blessed are those who mourn, for they shall be comforted. Blessed are the gentle, for they shall inherit the earth. Blessed are those who hunger and thirst for righteousness, for they shall be satisfied" (Matt. 5:3–6).

Jesus was describing the attitude of those who come to Him in true faith and repentance. They know they are bankrupt in spirit, so brokenhearted and mourning, meek and humble, and, having nothing to offer to accredit themselves, they hunger and thirst for righteousness alone. Those are the people who are only satisfied with Christ—they're the ones who receive the kingdom.

Psalm 34:18 says, "The Lord is near to the brokenhearted and saves those who are crushed in spirit." And again in Psalm 51:17, "The sacrifices of God are a broken spirit; a broken and a contrite heart, O God, You will not despise."

Denying yourself means realizing that nothing good resides in you (Rom. 7:18), that all your attempts at righteousness are nothing more than filthy rags (Isa. 64:6). Like the publican beating his chest, all you can do is cry out, "God, be merciful to me, the sinner!" (Luke 18:13).

Denying yourself is taking Christ on His terms, not yours. You offer no terms and no conditions. You cannot have Christ and your own pleasure, Christ and your own covetousness, or Christ and your own immorality. You come completely bankrupt, recognizing that you bring nothing to gain salvation.

---

1 Arthur Bennett, ed., *The Valley of Vision* (Edinburgh: Banner of Truth, 1975), Introductory Prayer.

From there you grow in grace, but it is, in a sense, growth downward. As you grow in the knowledge and the love of Christ, you form an increasingly lower estimation of yourself. It's a deepening realization of your utter unworthiness, a heartfelt recognition that you do not deserve His mercy. It's why Paul referred to himself as the "chief" of sinners (1 Tim. 1:15, NKJV). It's why he encouraged us to put aside our flesh and the old self, and renew our minds and new self in righteousness and holiness (Eph. 4:22–24).

And when you have truly died to self, you are fit for the work of the kingdom. You're unencumbered by the petty cares and concerns of this world. You're content with any food, any clothing, any climate, any social situation or solitude. You can put up with anything by the will of God.

It's when you never care to refer to yourself or point to your own good works; you're not chasing commendation, but content to be unknown and unrecognized. It's when you see a fellow believer prosper and have his or her needs met, and you can honestly rejoice, without a hint of envy and without questioning God on why you don't receive a similar blessing. It's when you can receive correction and reproof from one of less stature than yourself and humbly submit both inwardly and outwardly without rebellion or resentment. That's dying to self.

Jesus gave His disciples a second condition in Matthew 16:24. A follower of Christ must also be willing to "take up his cross." The meaning here is fairly plain. The cross was an instrument of torture and execution. It was a reprehensible device, intended for only the lowest and the vilest of society. It led to a gruesome, ghastly punishment—one of shame, humiliation, and public reproach; the mere thought of it would make most people shudder.

Christ was talking about death, and the worst kind of death, at that. The cross is not a metaphor you can apply to the various hardships of life. The cross is not your boss, it's not your neighbor, and it's not your mother-in-law. Jesus was talking about serious, sober things here. He was describing fierce persecution, up to the point of death.

Jesus had already warned His disciples about the potential cost of following Him. In Matthew 10:22 He told them, "You will be hated by all because of My name." But He also assured them of His loving care for His faithful servants.

> Do not fear those who kill the body but are unable to kill the soul; but rather fear Him who is able to destroy both soul and body in hell. Are not two sparrows sold for a cent? And yet not one of them will fall to the ground apart from your Father. But the very hairs of your head are all numbered. So

> do not fear; you are more valuable than many sparrows. Therefore everyone who confesses Me before men, I will also confess him before My Father who is in heaven. (10:28–32)

Taking up your cross means being willing to surrender your life. It means overruling your instinct for self-preservation. You surrender all concerns for your safety, protection, and well-being, knowing that your life resides in God's care, and that your eternity with Him is secure no matter what injuries or indignities the world might inflict on you.

It's the attitude Peter describes: "Beloved, do not be surprised at the fiery ordeal among you, which comes upon you for your testing, as though some strange thing were happening to you; but to the degree that you share the sufferings of Christ, keep on rejoicing, so that also at the revelation of His glory you may rejoice with exultation" (1 Pet. 4:12–13).

You might not face persecution unto death. But you need to be willing to surrender your life without hesitation if that's what the Lord requires of you.

Thirdly, Christ simply says, "Follow me" (Matt. 16:24). Or literally, "Let him be continually following Me." The life of a believer is a life of constant obedience. As Jesus said, "If you continue in My word, then you are truly disciples of Mine" (John 8:31). There are no cheat days in the Christian life—no time-outs and no hiatuses. As we've already seen, it is a life of self-denial. You have surrendered yourself to God, and you live in faithful obedience to His Word.

So this is the great contradiction. The Christian message is good news, but the good news begins by saying, "You have to deny yourself, be willing to give your life if the Lord asks for it, and set off on the narrow path, living a life of complete obedience to Christ." Or to put it more succinctly, you die and He lives in you.

Christ continued His sober statement with a warning. "For whoever wishes to save his life"—those who want to hold onto what they have—"will lose it; but whoever loses his life for My sake will find it" (Matt. 16:25).

The phrase "whoever loses his life" is synonymous with coming to Christ. The point again is simply that it will cost you. It will cost you your life and everything this temporal world has to offer. But by hanging onto those things, you are guaranteed to lose it forever. Nothing you grasp in this world will save you from judgment, and you can take nothing with you.

The Lord goes on to make that truth explicit. "For what will it profit a man if he gains the whole world and forfeits his soul? Or what will a man give in exchange for his soul?" (16:26). This contradicts the common understanding of the world—that the one with the most stuff is supposed to be the happiest.

Christ was showing the folly of such pursuits. A person could gain the whole world—he or she could amass all the power, accumulate all the wealth and material goods, he or she could fulfill all natural and carnal desires. But the person is still going to die, and nothing in his or her vast storehouses and deep pockets can buy back the person's soul when he or she faces God.

All the riches in the world are useless. There's not enough money in the world to buy your way out of judgment. No amount of power you can achieve can keep you out of an eternity in hell.

Those who put their faith in themselves and this life and all they can accumulate will lose it all. They will forfeit everything they were so desperate to gain. God's people live a great contradiction to this world, knowing that they can only gain life by surrendering it to Christ. We deny ourselves, take up our cross, and follow Him. And we plead with the people of this world to do likewise, that they might enjoy eternal life.

A Great Consummation

Finally, the church is distinguished by one last feature. In Matthew 16:27, Jesus said, "For the Son of Man is going to come in the glory of His Father with His angels, and WILL THEN REPAY EVERY MAN ACCORDING TO HIS DEEDS."

The church looks forward to the great consummation, which is the imminent return of our Lord. He will come to call His church out from the world and separate believers from unbelievers. Believers will enter into the joy of the Lord and the eternal bliss of heaven; unbelievers will face His fierce judgment and finally be cast into everlasting fire.

We already covered much of this ground in an earlier chapter, but let's consider it in the context of our passage. In light of the church's great contradiction, the Lord pointed His disciples' attention to His return and to the great consummation of all things. He reminded them that He would settle all accounts and that they would receive a reward for their lives of self-denial and suffering. He gave them the eternal good news that makes the temporary bad news insignificant. The hardships and trials of this life pale in comparison to the glories of heaven, and He wanted them to consider that along with everything He'd just told them about life in service to His kingdom.

This is the message of the church: self-denial, cross-bearing, and loyal obedience to Christ. That's not a message that many preachers are preaching today. But by way of encouragement, Jesus promised that He will return in glory of the Father and with His angels. And He promised them a preview. In Matthew 16:28 He added, "Truly I say to you, there are some of those who are standing here who will not taste death until they see the Son of Man coming in His kingdom."

Some have mistaken that to mean that the Second Coming happened within the lifetime of the disciples. But that's not what Christ was indicating. Rather, they were going to live long enough to see a preview of His second coming. They were going to see Him in His glory. And when did that happen?

In the very next verse, in chapter 17, we read, "Six days later Jesus took with Him Peter and James and John his brother, and led them up on a high mountain by themselves. And He was transfigured before them; and His face shone like the sun, and His garments became as white as light" (Matt. 17:1–2).

When you read the descriptions of coming judgment from the Olivet discourse and the book of Revelation, they're dominated by darkness. The whole universe essentially goes black. But Christ is returning in His glory like the blazing sun, robed in gleaming white. He showed His disciples a preview of His glorious second coming.

It says, "He was transfigured before them." He pulled aside the veil of His human flesh and revealed His blazing *shekinah*, or His divine glory. And if that wasn't enough of a foretaste, "Behold, Moses and Elijah appeared to them, talking with Him" (17:3). They also bore witness to their forefathers in the faith—great men who likewise denied themselves to follow God. And to top it all off, "A bright cloud overshadowed them, and behold, a voice out of the cloud said, 'This is My beloved Son, with whom I am well-pleased; listen to Him!'" (17:5). The Father Himself authenticated the message of the Son and the promise of His return.

The true church lives in light of Christ's return, and we warn people of the consummation to come. "Knowing the fear of the Lord, we persuade men" (2 Cor. 5:11), because when He comes, He is coming in judgment. The person who clings to this life will be a pauper forever, while the person who gives up this life—who abandons it to Christ—will reign forever as a prince in heaven. Every person must make that choice, and Christ's church urges all people to make it in light of His imminent return.

So in summary: How do you recognize a real church? It's not a matter of architecture. It's not about their rituals, traditions, liturgy, or worship style. It's not about whether it makes you feel good or if it's conveniently located.

You know it's a true church because you find people who are passionate about exalting the Lord Jesus Christ; who submit to the authority and sufficiency of Scripture; who understand the spiritual nature of the kingdom of salvation; who proclaim the cross and resurrection; who pursue holiness and purity in doctrine and practice; who are self-denying, humble, and obedient to the Word of God; and who live in anticipation of what is to come as promised by the Lord in His wonderful return.

That's what marks a true church. No wonder they're hard to find.

Study Questions:

1. What did the first-century Jews expect from the Messiah? How does the church today similarly try to shoehorn Jesus into what they want Him to be? How does the truth about Jesus differ from those expectations?
2. How does the death and resurrection of Christ shape the mission of the church?
3. What is the nature of Satan's opposition to God's purposes? How can you recognize a church that has joined Satan in this opposition?
4. Explain in your own words why the message of personal fulfillment that so many churches preach today is a problem.
5. How does the return of Christ motivate the church's faithfulness?

9

Why Membership Matters

WHAT'S SO IMPORTANT about your local church? In a time when there is more Bible teaching than you could ever consume available through radio, television, and the internet, why should it matter how or where you're taking in God's truth? What's wrong with virtual, web-based congregations for the digital-age church? Why can't you worship from the sanctuary of your smartphone?

The answer is simple: That's not the means God designed or decreed for His people to worship Him. We have not been called to an individualistic religion, shaped and defined by personal interests and tastes.

The Lord has a much loftier design for His church.

The New Testament repeatedly emphasizes the importance of local assemblies. In fact, it was the pattern of Paul's ministry to establish local congregations in the cities where he preached the gospel. Hebrews 10:24–25 commands every believer to be a part of such a local body and reveals why this is necessary: "Let us consider how to stimulate one another to love and good deeds, not forsaking our own assembling together, as is the habit of some, but encouraging *one another*; and all the more as you see the day drawing near."

The level of intimacy that is required to stimulate fellow believers "to love and good deeds" can only be cultivated in a gathered, local body. And only in this setting can we carry out the fullness of the "one-anothers" commanded in Scripture.

The New Testament also teaches that every believer is to be under the protection and nurture of local church leadership. These godly men can shepherd the believer by encouraging, admonishing, and teaching. Hebrews 13:7 and 17 help us to understand that God has graciously granted accountability to us through submission to godly leadership.

Furthermore, when Paul gave Timothy special instructions about believers' meetings, he said, "Give attention to the *public* reading of *Scripture*, to exhortation and teaching" (1 Tim. 4:13). Part of the emphasis in public worship includes these three things: hearing the Word, being called to obedience through exhortation, and teaching. These things can most effectively take place only in the context of the local assembly.

Consider again what Acts 2:42 tells us about the activities of the early church: "They were continually devoting themselves to the apostles' teaching and to fellowship, to the breaking of bread and to prayer." They learned God's Word and the implications of it in their lives, they joined to carry out acts of love and service to one another, they commemorated the Lord's death and resurrection through breaking bread, and they prayed.

Of course, we can do some of those things individually, but God has called us into His body, and we should gladly minister and be ministered to among God's people.

Active involvement in your local church is imperative to living a life without compromise. Only through the ministry of the local church can a believer receive the kind of teaching, accountability, and encouragement that is necessary for him to stand firm in his convictions. God has ordained that the church provides the fellowship in which an uncompromising life can thrive, and His people can grow spiritually.

Let's take a closer look at some of the fundamental functions of the church, and how they have a direct impact on our spiritual growth and our usefulness to the Lord. We'll also look at God's design for the church and how that design is part of the foundation of our spiritual lives.

Loving the Local Church

God's people need to remember that coming to Christ means coming to His church. As far back as the New Testament, salvation brought you into union with the visible, gathered body of Christ (Acts 2:47). Becoming a Christian meant entering fellowship with other Christians.

Tragically, that conviction has been lost in recent years. Contemporary evangelicalism emphasizes the believer's personal relationship to Christ. Individual faith is the pervasive theme, and you seldom hear discussion of how believers are supposed to fit together and function in the church.

When was the last time you read or heard a gospel presentation that ended with a discussion of the believer's relationship to the church? At best there is a very low emphasis on church involvement, church membership, and being a part of the family of God in the visible, gathered household of saints.

In the massive effort to make salvation personal, the church has been overlooked—to the detriment of many souls. Too many people today tend to be ecclesiastical consumers. They're only interested in what they can get out of their church, and they bounce from congregation to congregation or video sermon to sermon as their whims and interests change. They don't have any particular commitment or loyalty to a specific body of believers.

In fact, they have little to no attachment to the church at all. They are under no obligation to regularly attend—if they make it, they make it; if not, it's no big deal.

For people like that, their faith is solely defined personally; they have no corporate commitment or responsibility to the people of God. It's a skewed, unbalanced, and unbiblical pseudo-Christianity that exists completely outside of and apart from the body of Christ.

The idea of believers living independently of the church is totally foreign to the New Testament. The Holy Spirit addressed almost every epistle to a local church, and other books like First and Second Timothy, Titus, and Philemon were addressed to key leaders in local congregations. Even the book of James—which was written to believers scattered by persecution—assumes the recipients are still meeting together and deals heavily with life in the context of the church.

Throughout the New Testament, the assumption is always the same: that the people of God are faithfully gathering in a local assembly where the Word of God is dominant. That unified gathering—not just the invisible worldwide church, but also the local, visible congregation—is at the heart of true Christianity. The church is the only institution the Lord established and promised to bless.

Why would anyone who claims to love the Lord want to keep His people at arm's length?

Church Membership in the New Testament

Obviously, the leaders of the early church knew their flocks well. In Acts 20, Paul exhorted the elders of the Ephesian church to faithfully watch over and shepherd their people. But it's very difficult to shepherd if you don't know who your flock is. And sheep don't thrive just roaming around on their own.

Even though the New Testament never speaks of church membership in today's terms, the principles of life in the early church lay the foundation for faithfully submitting and belonging to a local congregation. While the original membership process might differ from today's patterns, no doubt New Testament Christians were lovingly bound to their local body of believers.

Peter's sermon on the day of Pentecost was a flashpoint in the explosive growth of the early church. Acts 2:41 says, "Those who had received his word were baptized; and that day there were added about three thousand souls."

Added to what? Added to the others. Acts 1:15 says that about 120 people were already gathered together in the upper room—the 3,000 people saved on the day of Pentecost would have been in addition to the core that already existed after Christ's ascension.

Their names might have been physically added to a list by someone keeping track, but that's not what is most important. The moment these men and women were saved, they were baptized as a visible testimony of their transformed lives and as a way to publicly identify with the other believers. They were immediately welcomed into the church fellowship.

Just a few verses later, Acts 2:47 says, "And the Lord was adding to their number day by day those who were being saved." The influx of new members didn't stop at Pentecost. The church met daily, and every day the Lord drew new men and women to Himself and into fellowship with His people.

And that growth wasn't merely short term. A few chapters later, in Acts 5:14, the church was still growing exponentially: "And all the more believers in the Lord, multitudes of men and women, were constantly added to *their number*." This implies that someone was keeping track of the ever-expanding size of the flock.

Of course, in the earliest days of the church, everyone met together. After Stephen's murder (Acts 7:54–60), believers were scattered by persecution. A church started in Antioch and then others began through Paul's ministry. Eventually the church extended in all directions through the apostles' missionary endeavors. What began with one massive congregation was reproducing itself from city to city as the teaching of the gospel spread and yet more men and women were saved.

But no matter where they were saved, the implication is that they were immediately welcomed into a local gathering of believers. In fact, any time someone moved or relocated, they brought with them, or were preceded by, letters of recommendation to their new congregation. Acts 18:27 describes how Apollos was commended to the church at Achaia by the disciples. It would have been typical to notify the church receiving him that he came with the blessing of his previous congregation.

Paul followed the same pattern. In Romans 16:1–2 he wrote, "I commend to you our sister Phoebe, who is a servant of the church which is at Cenchrea; that you receive her in the Lord in a manner worthy of the saints, and that you help her in whatever matter she may have need of you; for she herself has also been a helper of many, and of myself as well."

Phoebe's journey to Rome was no accident—she was probably the one who delivered Paul's letter to the church there. So at the end of his passionate epistle, he paused to make sure she was looked after and cared for by the believers in Rome. He was eager to keep track of his sheep, letting the other congregation know her faith was genuine.

He repeated this pattern with other epistles as well—and with good reason; the early church was very concerned to maintain its purity and to keep the tares out. Many factious, heretical, sinful people posed an immediate threat to the church. As genuine believers moved from place to place, authenticating their faith and their character helped protect the church from error, division, and corruption.

That protective attitude is appropriate. The Lord loves His church—He shed His blood and died for His church. We are His body in this world as He works through us to accomplish His will. And we are His bride in eternity, the object of His affection and love. He demands a chaste and pure bride.

One of the key ways the church can guard itself from error and maintain its purity is to confirm the faith of its people and keep them accountable. The early church didn't have a name for that—they didn't need one. Today, we call it church membership.

Membership Is Fellowship

The genuine spiritual unity of saved souls is evident throughout the New Testament. And back then, just as today, that unity was manifest in the local, Lord's Day gathering of believers.

Christians inherently bond together in shared spiritual life with those of similar faith. Through the new birth of salvation, we have entered a fellowship with other believers—a fellowship that's so wonderful, unique, and precious that Paul sternly warned the Corinthians to make sure they allowed no divisions among them that could threaten it (1 Cor. 1:9–10).

The Greek word we translate as fellowship (*koinōnia*) essentially means "partnership." Paul described that partnership in Galatians 2:9: "Recognizing the grace that had been given to me, James and Cephas and John, who were reputed to be pillars, gave to me and Barnabas the right hand of fellowship."

He and Barnabas were affirmed and welcomed into common participation in eternal life, as it is manifest through the visible life of the church.

That's exactly what happens in church membership: The individual believer is publically identified with the local body of believers and enters an ongoing spiritual partnership with that congregation. It's a public affirmation of our unity in Christ, our care for each other, and our shared desire to grow together in the love and knowledge of God's Word.

That's why the modern trend of believers floating freely between congregations and never firmly planting in one place is a foreign concept to Scripture. Our model today is built on a consumer mentality—people go to church wherever their felt needs are addressed, only to unplug and move on when those needs change or are better met somewhere else. That pattern is completely contrary to the one we find in God's Word.

In fact, Scripture expressly forbids this fluidity. Hebrews 10:23–25 is unequivocal regarding the necessity of fellowship.

> Let us hold fast the confession of our hope without wavering, for He who promised is faithful; and let us consider how to stimulate one another to love and good deeds, not forsaking our own assembling together, as is the habit of some, but encouraging *one another*; and all the more as you see the day drawing near.

How can the people of God "stimulate one another to love and good deeds" if they aren't regularly meeting together? It can't happen. Forsaking the consistent fellowship of other believers cuts you off from a key, God-ordained source of biblical instruction, refining accountability, and spiritual growth (Prov. 27:17).

And the need for fellowship is even greater as we draw nearer to the return of Christ. The shepherdless flock won't thrive; it will scatter. Lone sheep are easy prey for wolves. Faithful fellowship helps insulate you from the influences of a world that's sprinting to hell. Why wouldn't a Christian take advantage of that?

Instead, too many believers today approach church like a duty or a task—one that's quickly pushed aside and forgotten as soon as it's been accomplished.

I can't understand that attitude. I want to be with the people of God every opportunity I get. I want to share together in our common love for the Lord and His truth. I want to build and deepen friendships, bear each other's burdens, and extend comfort and encouragement to those who need it. I want to come together with a collective choir of believers to sing praises to the Lord. I want to pray and worship with people who love

God's Word, and I want to see firsthand what His Word is accomplishing in their lives.

All of that is meant to happen in the church—not outside of it.

Membership Is Submission

As a pastor, I know I will have to give an account for the people under my leadership (Heb. 13:17). Every pastor faces the same burden for the souls under his care. But what good is a shepherd if the sheep won't submit to his authority? In an age of unprecedented ecclesiastical consumerism, how can a pastor lead, serve, or even know a flock that is inconsistent and fluctuating?

Active involvement in and submission to a local church body is crucial if we're going to live up to God's plan and pattern for the church. As we've already seen, the idea of Christians floating free between multiple congregations and never committing to one church body is completely alien to the New Testament. That kind of untethered independence cuts you off from the authority the Lord established through His church.

But just what that authority looks like is the cause of much controversy in the church today. Some pastors exercise illegitimate authority over their churches, with a level of involvement in their members' lives that borders on abusive or dictatorial. It's not the pastor's role to tell his people where they should live, where they should work, whom they should marry, or to exert that kind of control in other areas of their lives.

The only biblical authority a pastor has comes from the Word of God and the Holy Spirit working through his teaching in the lives of his flock. In effect, he's not a source of authority himself, but a conduit from the Lord to His people. That's the authority God's people need to submit to—the work of the Spirit through the faithful, consistent teaching of God's Word.

And how should believers respond to that kind of authority? A closer look at Hebrews 13:17 gives us the answer. "Obey your leaders and submit to them, for they keep watch over your souls as those who will give an account. Let them do this with joy and not with grief, for this would be unprofitable for you."

Trying to shepherd a rebellious flock is a burdensome grief. Watching over the people of God is no easy task. Pastors are called to train, disciple, support, and serve the church. We're also called to exhort, warn, admonish, reprove, rebuke, and discipline in the application of God's Word in believers' lives—all for the sake of their spiritual growth.

That's hard enough with believers who are eager and engaged in the process. It's impossible with people who won't be faithful to the flock and who want little to do with your leadership.

If you have a faithful pastor or church leaders who exemplify the qualities of a shepherd, let them know how much you appreciate their labor on your behalf (1 Thess. 5:12). It will be a great encouragement for them to know they're making a spiritual difference in your life.

And if you're a believer who has been rejecting the biblical authority of the local church and won't submit to your pastor or church leaders, you need to do a careful, thorough examination of your heart. What's behind your rebellious spirit? What sins are you harboring that are keeping you from submitting to God-given authority? Are you sure you truly belong to Christ?

The true authority of the church isn't harsh, impersonal, or oppressive. It's parental—building you up and working for your benefit (1 Thess. 2:7–12). Don't be foolish enough to reject that kind of biblical influence and authority in your life. Seek it out and submit to it in church membership.

Membership Is Identity

Our society is suffering from an identity crisis. Collectively and individually, people don't have a strong sense of who they are or what they should pursue. They drift anchorlessly through life, following the whims and fads of the world instead of accepting responsibility and pursuing maturity.

Christians don't need to struggle with that kind of identity crisis. We've been redeemed and claimed by Christ, brought into His family, and are being transformed into His likeness. To some degree, it should be difficult to tell where He stops and where you start, so to speak. As Paul says in Galatians 2:20, "I have been crucified with Christ; and it is no longer I who live, but Christ lives in me."

That glorious truth describes the spiritual state of every believer. We are no longer isolated and alone—the Lord bought us with a price (1 Cor. 6:20) and grafted us into His family (Rom. 11:17). We bear His name, and our transformed lives are a testimony to His love and power. Christ's sacrifice on our behalf establishes our new identity for eternity—we are His church, His body, and His bride.

But if we are individually identified with Christ, why, then, do so many Christians refuse to identify with the church—a collection of others likewise identified with the Savior? Why do they refuse church membership and reject fellowship with a local congregation? If the Lord has made us all one family in eternity, why do so many believers spend so much time here on earth avoiding one another?

Paul sternly warned Timothy to not be ashamed of the testimony of the Lord (2 Tim. 1:8). In his case, Timothy had real reasons to be afraid of publicly proclaiming his faith and identifying with the church: He faced the constant threat of physical persecution, imprisonment, and even death.

Most believers today will never face that kind of pressure. Instead, the resistance to identifying with the church is born out of a different kind of fear of humans. In our perpetually shallow and increasingly atheistic culture, nothing is cool about the church. So rather than being saddled with the stigma of stodgy religion, some professing believers try to discreetly live out their faith through loose affiliation with one—and sometimes more than one—congregation. Others just avoid the church altogether, ashamed that anyone might think they belong.

The idea of giving in to that kind of meager pressure would be laughable if so many Christians weren't doing it every day. But rather than proudly and publicly uniting with other believers, they chase fickle popular approval.

Others avoid binding themselves to a local congregation in an attempt to fly under the radar, fearing identification with God's people would lead to the exposure of things they want hidden.

What you do in the matter of church fellowship says a lot about the true state of your heart. The best indication of your priorities is how and where you spend your time and energy. Perhaps you're part of a political movement, a school board, a neighborhood committee, a fan club, or some other pursuit.

Of all the organizations you could belong to, the church is not optional. Your commitment to and identification with your local congregation speaks volumes about who you are and what matters most to you. In fact, your participation in your church is so much more than a once- or twice-weekly activity; it's a gathering of people who are no longer citizens of this world, a fellowship of men and women who have been transformed into new creatures and united in faith. As we saw in previous chapters, the church is a foretaste of the glories that await us in eternity. It is heaven on earth.

So if you claim to love the Lord but refuse to identify with His people, it raises understandable questions about the veracity of your love. At the same time, if your reputation with the unsaved world means enough to keep you away from the church, you have cause for serious concerns about whether you've truly repented and believed in the first place.

One other thing to consider when it comes to reputations: It's true that you could suffer in some circles if you publicly identify with your local church. It might even prove humiliating for you.

But that's nothing compared to the humiliations Christ willingly and sacrificially suffered on our behalf. And if the Lord is willing to associate Himself with weak, sinful people like us, we can't keep Him or His church at arm's length. If He's not ashamed to call us His, we cannot be ashamed to call Him—and His—ours.

Membership Is Loyalty

By now it should be clear that local church membership is crucial. Admittedly, no verse in the Bible specifically commands us to sign on the dotted line and join a church. But the clear teaching of Scripture is that we are to be members in the local fellowship of believers, in every sense of the word.

The apostle Paul had that unified fellowship in mind when he wrote Ephesians 2:19, "So then you are no longer strangers and aliens, but you are fellow citizens with the saints, and are of God's household." In essence, we're now part of a family—God's family.

And unity within God's heavenly household requires loyalty, both to Him and to His people. The consumerist attitude that's taken hold in the church today isn't interested in loyalty. It leads people to see relationships as a means to selfish ends—they will meet with other believers, but only when it suits their needs and pleases their interests.

When you come to church, the question shouldn't be, "What can I get out of my church?" but, "How can God use me to serve others here?" Will other believers in the congregation need you—whether for help, support, or encouragement?

The obvious answer is yes. There is no shortage of spiritual, physical, and emotional needs in your church. You won't have to look hard to find many ways you can be useful to your congregation. It's the same attitude you'd hope to cultivate within your own family—What are the needs around you, and how can you help meet those needs? Bring that loyal, Christlike attitude with you to church—you're not there to be served, but to serve.

By God's grace and His perfect design, He has equipped each of us with a variety of spiritual gifts for use in the church (Eph. 4:11–12). The Lord has fitted each of us with specific talents and abilities that tie into His purposes for our lives.

Every believer has a role within the body of Christ, and that body cannot fully function unless everyone is working together (1 Cor. 12:12–31). Hands can't suddenly become ears; eyes can't replace feet. And you'll never find a stray finger or tongue that functions better on its own than it does with the rest of the body. The Lord didn't save us to be solo acts—we're meant to work in concert and harmony together as one great choir.

How is that possible apart from involvement in the local church? You may have other believers scattered throughout your life, whether at home, at work, or elsewhere. But God's design is for you to be an active, useful member of your local church body, serving in love side by side with other useful, self-sacrificing believers to accomplish His will in your individual lives and in your collective community. That starts with being a loyal member of your local assembly of our Lord's church.

Study Questions:

1. Where do we see church membership in the New Testament?
2. What causes people to be reluctant to join a church?
3. What does true fellowship with other believers involve?
4. How does our identity in Christ relate to church membership?
5. Explain in your own words why commitment to a local body of believers is so important.

Fort Washington, PA 19034

This book is published by CLC Publications, an outreach of CLC Ministries International. The purpose of CLC is to make evangelical Christian literature available to all nations so that people may come to faith and maturity in the Lord Jesus Christ. We hope this book has been life changing and has enriched your walk with God through the work of the Holy Spirit. If you would like to know more about CLC, we invite you to visit our website:

www.clcusa.org

To learn more about the remarkable story of the founding of CLC International, we encourage you to read

LEAP OF FAITH

Norman Grubb
Paperback
Size 5¼ x 8, Pages 248
ISBN: 978-0-87508-650-7
ISBN (*e-book*): 978-1-61958-055-8